Destination Joy:

A guidebook to feeling good

Linda L. Fallucca, Ph.D, MSC.D.

Published by Fallucca Publishing, Northbrook, Illinois   www.lindafallucca.com

Printed in the United States of America.

Cover design by Richard Koranda   SR Koranda Advertising, Inc.

Library of Congress Cataloging-in-Publication Data
Fallucca, Linda Destination Joy: A guidebook to feeling good/Linda Fallucca
1. Spiritual life 2. Personal Development 3. Meditation 4. Title
ISBN 0-9724524-1-9   10 9 8 7 6 5 4 3 2 1   First July 2005 $13.95

Acknowledgements

To Abraham, and to Jerry and Esther Hicks, I offer my appreciation and my love for your wonderful words and encouragement, and most of all, your friendship.

To Cynthia Sutherland, Gail Lawrence and Carolyn Sodini, I deeply thank you; without your assistance this surely would still be a work in progress.

To Rich Koranda, thank you for your beautiful artwork, your time and your vision.

I also wish to express much appreciation to my family, and to the many who have lent their time, their assistance and their support to this project. You have made it all flow so much more easily.

My love to you all.

Table of Contents

Destination Joy: A guidebook to feeling good

Introduction–   Page 1

Chapter 1   Page 15
Creating Joy for You, With Linda and Abraham–
Getting Ready to Fly

Chapter 2   Page 19
The Path to Creating (Universal Laws)–Establishing
Your Flight Plan

Chapter 3   Page 26
The True Cause of Turbulence–Delays in the
Friendly Skies

Chapter 4   Page 37
Appreciation and Unconditional Love–Flying First Class

Chapter 5   Page 42
Health, Wealth and Relationships–Frequent Flyers

Chapter 6   Page 48
Energy Flowing Tools–The Mechanics of Maintenance

Chapter 7   Page 68
Putting It All Together–A Joyful Journey

Chapter 8   Page 75
Happy Landings

Addendum   Page 86
Thoughts from Linda

Glossary   Page 120

Resource Guide Page 125
Linda Fallucca and Abraham-Hicks Web-Sites

Introduction

Life is a journey–it's like a trip, or a vacation. You start out with joyful anticipation as you head towards your destination. You expect that everything along the way will be fun and joyous, and your dreams and plans include wanting everything to go smoothly. You want no delays, and no unexpected events. Your journey should be the dream vacation, from beginning to end. Like a television commercial, you will be transported from the start directly to your destination. And then you find that vacations–and life–are not always like that.

You have heard this in so many ways: "The joy is in the journey." You may have picked up this book because you really want more joy in your life. More fun. More appreciation. More good stuff! But how do you get it? How do you get from "here" to "there"?

This book is about getting more of the joy you want, and being easy with yourself along the way. And this book is not a "how to," it's a guide. Only you can create the joy you want.

There is nothing more frustrating than having someone tell you that, "You create your own reality," because when you look around at your body, your job, your relationships, or something that isn't working, you usually say, "Hey, I didn't want that. I couldn't have created this thing."

And that's when you say, "It's just much easier to blame someone else for what isn't going right in my life. I can't accept the responsibility for creating something I have that I don't like. It can't be my fault."

Well, the good news is: it's not your fault. The rest of the news is: you really did create it, but you don't get the blame. In a vibrational Universe, there is no blame. You usually create by default, by not knowing how you are vibrating or how you are creating what you are creating. Why? It's very likely that no one taught you about vibrations and energies when you started your life, so you create by vibrating in certain ways without knowing that's how you're creating what is coming to you.

"Wait," you say. "I'm a beginner with this information. Just what is this vibrational Universe that I'm living in?" Good question, fellow traveler, since even those of us who've logged lots of spiritual miles struggle with this concept quite often.

Let me explain about "vibration." People who have studied advanced physics and physiology understand that we are physically composed of matter that manifests chemically as energy. It's not always easy to think of our bones and skin and thoughts and feelings as energy; but, basically, that is how you are put together.

How you flow or express this energy is what we are calling "vibration." It is not just how you use or flow your energy, but how you interpret through your feelings what is happening around you, too.

Introduction

Vibrations are the basis for what attracts you to certain people and things, to certain sports and activities. While the Source of energy is the same for everyone, each person's expression of it is different. That's why we call it "flowing your energy." It is the basis for all your creativity and choice. It is why everyone is different, even though we all stem from the same Source. Vibrations are how you feel, and how you feel is what directs your creative process.

So, if you are a beginner, or even a seasoned traveler in the thoughts that you are in a vibrational Universe that holds more than just promises, i.e., you believe that it holds your creative fulfillment, then this book is a boarding pass for your journey, but not a seat assignment. You have many choices to make on this trip. If you have been a "spiritual" student of many years (and a veteran of seminars and workshops and many long distance flights), there is something in here for you, too. We are all lifelong students.

If you want to know how to deliberately create what you want and to feel joy, then come on this journey with me. Think of this book as a guide to your personal flight. The destinations, and the stops along the way, are your choice. There are no restrictions on age, sex, political or religious inclinations. I am personally excited about the journey that lies ahead of you. To journey with me in this guidebook, you need to pack light. So, here is the most important stuff. *3*

1. *Leave all guilt behind.*

Throw it out. Don't take it with you, because you don't need it any more. I don't care where you got your guilt from: a Jewish mom, a Catholic mother, a Protestant parent, in a Moslem culture, your society, a teacher, or a friend. Leave it behind. It is useless baggage. It doesn't fit any longer. There is an important statement made by my friend Abraham: "You never get it wrong, and you never get it done." I'll explain who Abraham is later. Pack this statement, but leave guilt out. If you haven't liked what you have created in the past, don't worry about it.

2. *Leave blame behind.*

I said it before, but it bears repeating. Blame is the bane of the Universe. The more you use it, the more you lose. And the more "old stuff" you drag along with you, the "heavier" you feel. You don't need the entire plane, just one seat, so blame has to go. Since there is a baggage limit on this trip, blame belongs in the "overweight" baggage compartment.

3. *Definitely DO pack your sense of humor.*

When Abraham says, "You never get it wrong, and you never get it done," I say that your sense of humor is very important in the creating process. As Thomas Edison learned so well, it took a few jolts and some static on the way to discovering electricity. And, a few jolts and some static are part of the fun as long as you don't stall and stay in that part of the creative process.

You just have to laugh at yourself, and with others. Lighten up. One carry-on bag is allowed per passenger, so put your sense of humor in it! Life always seems to offer a few jolts; that's what keeps it interesting, and it allows you to refine. Your sense of humor softens those jolts (the contrast).

4. Be prepared to love every destination on this journey of life.
It may not be the most exciting city or hotel you've stayed in, but there is always something good about each stop. Look for it, it's called appreciation, and "Appreciation" gets its own chapter (Chapter 4).

5. Be open to change.
Life is not a fixed itinerary. And neither is the creative process.

6. Do pack your most positive thoughts and feelings.
So it's really close to you at all times, put two additional important ingredients in your *carry-on bag* for this journey of your lifetime. It may seem strange at first, but as you move forward, you'll understand why. These two additional items are your thoughts and feelings. How you feel and what you think will have a lot to do with what happens to you. Well, not just a lot, but everything that happens to you. I mention "what you think" and "how you feel" early on in this guide-book because these are the two most important items of your journey.

Do you believe that your thoughts and feelings create your destiny? Do you believe that you are the creator of your own experience?

I DO! And, I will have a great deal to say about your thoughts and feelings as we move along.

Getting on board... Before I introduce you to the crew in the cockpit of your plane, there are a few other things to be said first. I have already introduced the words "vibrational Universe" and "the importance of your thoughts and feelings." And, I've mentioned that you are the creator of your own reality on your lifetime journey. I've used the word "spiritual." You now have the idea that we are going to be talking about the inner you, and discussing topics and ideas that sometimes make the most creative and intelligent people leery, if not uncomfortable, but please bear with me.

In this modern world, even with media attention to the contrary, there is still a feeling of discomfort about anything that cannot be physically "nailed down" in a textbook. I want to give you a comfort level before starting because I consider this information to be so very important to you. I think this is all information you have heard before in various ways and from various authors and teachers, but how you receive the information and then process it, is of utmost importance.

All of the great teachers and philosophers have received their information from somewhere. Moses didn't have the Library of Congress at his disposal when he brought the tablets with the Ten Commandments to his people.

Every prophet and philosopher and religion developer had to have some source that was outside the written and spoken information of the day. And, it is here that faith in your own inner knowing, as well as faith in your own mind and logical thinking, comes into play.

If all important information came from "somewhere" in the beginning, what was the source, and why and how was the information accessed and then given to the rest of the world as the written and spoken word? Is it perhaps because we are truly "all connected," and is it possible that information outside of today's media is available to you from an inner Source? I think so, and I also think that you have the ability to receive and process this information, if you have faith in your own inner power. So with that, meet your crew.

*The crew...*By way of introduction, I want you to know and be in tune with the crew that is with you in this guidebook. You can think of the crew more as a staff of teachers as well as guides, and you must count yourself in as a "teacher" also, so start now to think of yourself as part of the crew, even as you get a better sense of understanding your role.

All teachers have teachers, and our "teacher of teachers" will be a non-physical entity or group that is known today as "Abraham"–a group that has brought their message to us via Esther and Jerry Hicks of San Antonio, Texas. This group, Abraham, is not to be confused with the Abraham of the Old Testament of the Bible.

I want you to think of Abraham, momentarily, as an enormous conglomerate that has made itself known in response to the quest of humanity to better understand who they are and why they are here. It will be a little difficult, at first, to think of yourself as a member of that conglomerate, but I am going to ask you to do just that.

7

So often you put your highest hopes and beliefs into something outside of yourself, as if you have no part in the controls or actions of the world around you. Abraham is a source that helps you understand and appreciate your participation in life and your role with God, Source or All That Is, or whatever term you choose to assign to the creative process, including your ability to be in your body, and on this earth.

I will have more to say about Abraham as we proceed, but for now, it is only important that you think of Abraham as the Master Teacher, and the rest of your crew as the "hands on" group to assist you on your journey. As the author of this guidebook, I'll be your captain, your primary teacher, so let's begin.

A message from your captain... I am here to assist you with your journey through life, using this book as a guide, because I believe that a joyous life experience is something that you want, and that the desire to be joyous is what binds us together. It is what we all have in common. I believe we came into this life knowing that a joyous life was not only possible, but probable.

I want to share with you information that I believe you already "know" but have temporarily forgotten–about flowing energy, about vibrations, about the nature of thought, and about the use of feelings. I believe that you know, on some level, that you have an "inner being," a spiritual part that recognizes you as more than just a body.

Sharing my own early journey... Teaching and counseling and writing and working with individuals about their spiritual energy have been my life's work. While much of what I have done might look impressive to some people, it might be amusing to you to know that I attribute most of my early learning and experiences about energies to my childhood.

My early years could have been considered lonely and isolated, but I didn't experience this time that way at all. Even though I was alone most of the time, I spent my days blissfully in nature: under the open sky, in vast fields, walking or sitting along quiet streams and majestic woods. I grew up in beautiful surroundings. I now recognize that much of my time was spent in a meditative state, appreciating everything all around me.

I genuinely believe that we arrive on this earth with a knowing about our connection to the spiritual, and that many of us lose this connection along the way with the admonitions of others to "live in reality," "don't daydream," or "don't be idle." As a very young child I was given a lot of time to spend in nature, and became aware that I could see and feel the energy in the trees, in flowers, and in animals as well as in people–that was *my* reality.

I always had a "knowing" that I was a non-physical being as well as a physical one, and that I was connected to all of those trees and animals, as well as to people. I easily felt the energy around me, and actually thought that everyone else could feel and see as I did, too.

9

As you might guess, everyone thought of me as "psychic," and also a bit "different," as they began to think of me as unlike themselves. This occurred because, by simply reading the energies they were emitting, I knew what was going on with peoples' lives. Over time, I learned not to freely share with others what I saw–and felt–and sensed–because it made them uncomfortable.

Most people I interacted with were only comfortable thinking I was "different," that I had a "gift," or that I was someone who could tell them what was happening or would happen in their lives. They didn't want to hear that what I was "seeing" were really energy patterns that they themselves created–patterns that could ebb and flow with their thoughts and emotions. They didn't want to hear that they had the ability to change their lives themselves through being aware of and refining their vibrations. They definitely didn't want to hear that my ability was something that they also possessed–something that they had just forgotten how to use.

I began my own practice many years ago, seeing individuals, facilitating seminars and teaching my knowing. My desire to find new words to explain what I knew became a burning desire, and it didn't surprise me that such a focused desire would be answered by the Universe.

Sometime in the late 1980's, at the height of my desire, someone sent me a tape, and I was introduced to the teachings of Abraham via Esther Hicks and her husband, Jerry Hicks. It was one of those wonderful moments you get in life when your heart just sings and you know you have connected with what feels right. Your heart and mind just "know" it is right. I truly had "come home" with words to explain my lifelong knowing.

In their tapes, Abraham via Esther described how we all create our reality by allowing or disallowing the non-physical energy, and it was this knowing that has brought this book to fruition. Everything that I had felt as a child and had expanded upon as an adult was brought together in one glorious thought process for me.

And now, after more than a decade of using what I learned and lived, and combining it with the teachings of Abraham, I want to share it with you because I believe, even more strongly now, that life is a joyous journey–and you are endowed with the creativity of All That Is to live your life in joy and happiness. Let me guide you in bringing together all that you know, and all that I know, and which Abraham has clarified for us in our journey, to create a joyful life.

My intention with this book is to share with you the knowledge, and the knowing, not only of what I have experienced, but what I have also witnessed with my clients and students. I want to share my reflections about how you can take your thought beyond anything you have understood before.

Through the sharing in this guidebook, my wish for you would be to use this information to create your own joyous life experience. Likewise, my intent is to continue refining my own knowing, attracting more new avenues of joy.

Since everything is energy, the quality of your life reflects how you are tapping into and flowing that energy. The most important principle for you to learn and understand is to consciously tap into and connect with that energy to create the life you want.

Introduction

You can experience a magnificent life–right here on earth–by allowing the fullness of who you are.

This process is a very personal thing and everyone must do it for themselves, in their own way. But, it is vital to fully comprehend that you are an extension of the non-physical, spiritual energy, and then learn how to recognize when you are in vibrational harmony with that energy. The *missing link* would be: not allowing the energy of your Inner Being (your soul…the non-physical, spiritual you, your connection to the Source, the Universal energy) to flow through you.

*And so, our guidebook…*The theme of this book is about "creating"–creating more joy in your life. Each chapter examines aspects of the creative process. It is a travel manual that I hope will trigger your unique knowing into remembering that you knew how to fly all the time!

Chapter 1:
The stage is set for our journey, and, the journey is about how you seek and create joy throughout your lifetime. You get ready by focusing on thoughts and feelings that make you feel good.

Chapter 2:
Here we establish our flight plan, with the Universal laws that govern all creative activity. Like gravity, these rules apply to us all, no one gets around them. They are the basis of all creation, the foundation for your flight through life.

Chapter 3:
We will discuss here how we get in our own way. Turbulence isn't always a bad thing, but you don't need it for the entire trip.

Chapter 4:
There is nothing better than flying first class. There are two things that will always get you there. Don't skip this chapter!

Chapter 5:
The frequent flyers of our life experience are health, wealth and relationships. It seems we never fly alone!

Chapter 6:
You can avoid mechanical break downs; this is the tool box designed to keep the emergencies of lifetime travel at a minimum.

Chapter 7:
We put it all together in a fantasy trip to see if we can pack, wrinkle-free!

Chapter 8:
And then we look at the endless path of creation and creativity. How do you view this and what else is out there to make your travel plans smoother?

And for dessert, I provide an **Addendum** of some of my bi-monthly "Thoughts from Linda" for you to use as little "mental fresheners" as you continue on your creative and glorious life adventure. There is also a very short **Resource Guide** to assist you.

Read and enjoy what you find here and be open to new ideas that may not be familiar to you. But rest assured, these ideas will change your perspective, and hopefully, let you enjoy your time here in the physical reality more fully.

Finally, there is a **Glossary** of terms, for all the reasons we ever use a glossary!

 one

Creating joy for you,
with Linda and Abraham–
Getting Ready To Fly

Think thoughts that make you feel good...Speak words that make you feel good...Get the feeling of how you would like your life to be...Get the feeling as if you are already living that life.

Thoughts from Linda

If this book has found its way into your hands, then I am pretty certain that you are among the many people who are feeling, especially at this time on our planet, that we play a role in the creation of our happiness.

You could be new to this or you may be one who has read many books and attended many seminars on how to use your mind for good health, unlimited wealth and an abundance of good things. You may also be among those who sink to despair and confusion when you don't create the perfect life in thirty days or less.

You could be the eternal optimist. Or you could even be one of those who have, at times, just "given up" and said, "Someone or something else is to blame for my unhappiness," or "It's my karma," or "It's my Mom (or Dad)." Maybe you just gave up thinking you ever would have the joyful life that you desire, that only those with "luck" could achieve their goals.

15

Wherever you are in the scheme of things, most people have "been there," and yet somehow they have this "knowing" that urges them on.

I believe that you are the creator of your own experience. I believe that your thoughts and feelings create your destiny. I also believe that on some level, you know that everything is about energies, vibrations and your connection to Source–by how you think and feel. Those energy signals are sent out to the Universal broadcasting system and are manifested accordingly.

In my own spiritual journey, I am always refining, growing and changing. And, I find it fascinating and exciting that Abraham keeps expanding the message also.

So here we are, you with your desires and wanting for a happy life, and me with my desire for you to create a happy life by sharing with you what I have known, what I feel, and how my association with Abraham has refined my knowing. So, who is Abraham and how does this all fit together here? I described who Abraham is in my Introduction: a "group" of non-physical teachers who chose to speak through Esther Hicks because of the purity and clarity of her as a physical vehicle, and because of the powerful focus and desire for knowing of her husband, Jerry Hicks. Now, I want to share why Abraham is so important to me in the context of this guidebook.

When I was thinking about writing this book, I had a series of conversations with Abraham through Esther Hicks. I spoke to Abraham about how to use the Abraham-like words I often use in my teachings, seminars and workshops and how to acknowledge incorporating those words into this book. I am aware that I teach and explain my knowing to others with an easier flow of words now because of the refining and clarity that Abraham's words have given me about the energies and vibrations I interpret.

In addition, I am in alignment with what Abraham says is the most meaningful and important part of their message: that you need to understand your connection to the Source energy; that you are an extension of All That Is; that guidance is within you at every moment through your Inner Being if you allow that connection to flow; and, this is the constant energy stream of knowing.

Abraham encouraged me to write this book, and said that communication is more about energy than anything else. This means that you respond to others by what you feel from each other's vibrations. We really are in this physical world together, communicating in many ways, not just by our speech or our specific words, but by the way we vibrate.

Abraham said that when you find words that others have agreed upon and you express those words in a way that promotes pure, positive energy, those meaningful and well-applied words can interpret for others in a way that brings about true knowing. The knowing occurs because the words are inspired and resonate with peoples' awareness vibrationally.

Words are a vehicle to receive the energy transmission, similar to someone who is learning a language. When you were a child, for example, and your mother pointed to something and said the word at the same time, you made the association.

In effect, Abraham said that I was receiving the non-physical transmission at the same time that I was hearing his words, so those words have become the best choice of a label to assist me in explaining to others about the essence, and the energy.

And so, I want to note that throughout this book, I often use Abraham's words to explain the energies and vibrations, as translated and published by Esther and Jerry Hicks. I am so at one with Abraham's teachings, and Esther's translation of Abraham, that it's difficult to separate my knowing from Abraham's words. But, I accept that this book reflects my own unique knowing, combined with my interpretation of Abraham. The thoughts expressed here are my creative responsibility, even though our life adventures are always the product of co-creation!

 Two

The path to creating
(Universal Laws)–
Establishing your Flight Plan

YOU *are the creator–you get to create your own destination*

If you want to change what you're living, you only have to change the balance of your thoughts and feelings. As you think, you feel; as you feel, you vibrate; and, what you're vibrating is what you're creating.

Abraham-Hicks

If we all made the path to creating as simple as it really is, we'd all be living such joyous lives that there would be no need for this book or any kind of teachers. But we humans love the joy of creation, so sometimes we make the process more complicated than it really is. I like to think that we do it just for the fun of the creating, but the truth is that we tend to make a simple plan anything but simple.

The Universe has very few laws, but there are some. These are laws that cannot be changed or rewritten. They are the beginning and the end of our creative process. They are so ingenious, so beautifully intended, that it is amazing that three laws could govern all that we are and all that we want to be.

19

They are not new laws. They have been written and spoken about in some way or another for quite some time. One of Abraham's greatest contributions was to offer this information in a way that enabled our ability to understand these laws better and to integrate them into everyday living. The laws are in action during your entire journey, even if you're not aware of their existence.

These laws are:

1. *The Law of Attraction.*
2. *The Law of Deliberate Creation.*
3. *The Law of Allowing.*

We'll examine them one at a time, but please remember that they overlap, are intertwined, and that these laws do not stand alone in the classic sense. They exist with and for each other. They may be defined separately, but they do not operate independently.

The first law, which is the basis for the second two laws, is:

The Law of Attraction.
The Law of Attraction is best defined by this progression of activities: "As we think, we feel. As we feel, we vibrate. What we vibrate, we create." More simply put, you are the attractor of your experience. This law means simply that you are always creating, no matter what. What you are creating is based upon how you are flowing your energy. So, you are always attracting, whether you are doing it intentionally or not. You are attracting with your feelings and your thoughts.

Therefore, whatever thoughts and feelings you think and feel are the vibrations you send out, and that's what comes back to you.

You've heard the phrase, "Like is attracted to like," and, "As you sow, so shall you reap." You have heard these comments many times before. They are variations on how people have understood this basic law.

What this means is that whatever you give your attention to, or whatever you think about, and whatever you feel, will draw more of the same things to you. It means that you really are the attractor of your experience. No one else in the Universe has anything to do with what you bring to you.

Does this mean that if you have an uncomfortable or angry thought or feeling that it will bring something "bad" to you immediately? No. The Universe is incredibly wise and it has provided you with a powerful "guidance" system. That guidance system is your emotions.

If that seems confusing, please remember that you were not taught about this guidance system as a very small child, and many of us have learned how to interpret our emotions differently, through habit. But, your emotions exist, and they support you in your creative process in a very powerful and good way.

Later on in this guidebook, we will go over how to reacquaint yourself with this powerful tool for your happiness. I introduce this to you now so that you don't become too uncomfortable or fearful.

I will also elaborate later on the fact that you can't ever "get it wrong" and you also never "get all your creating done." So, just see this extraordinary Law of Attraction as powerful, but loving. Learning to understand this law and using it wisely is the basis for the next law.

Law of Deliberate Creation

This law is exactly what it says, creating deliberately by deliberately choosing both what you give your attention to and how you feel. It is a deliberate decision to create something by putting yourself in vibrational alignment with that decision to make it happen. You choose the direction of your thoughts and feelings. You choose what to focus on. You choose what to filter out of your environment and your thoughts. It is about wanting and then making your own clear choice.

There is a process to deliberate creation, and that process includes the Law of Attraction. The manifestation of what you want is linked to the third law. So I will explain the third law next and then put them all together for you.

Law of Allowing

This is one of the more difficult laws to explain and for most people to put into use. This law is also often the hardest one for people to manage.

You know what you want; you have deliberately stated it to the Universe; and you have felt the promise of what you want. But now you have to know and trust and allow yourself to receive what you want. You have to get out of your own way by feeling good.

This is the law that trips us up the most, and sometimes makes us feel like we don't have input into creating our reality. And this is the law that often turns us into momentary unbelievers.

What is important here is to understand that you have become accustomed to trying to control the events in your life. You have had an inclination to "worry" along the process of what you want. And you question when it doesn't arrive as quickly as you want.

What is allowing like? What does being an "allower" mean? An allower must first really understand the Law of Attraction. An allower is one who comprehends how you create deliberately in your experience. But most of all, an allower is one who does not give attention to those things not wanted. Allowing is being in alignment with you–with the Source energy–the life stream. Allowing means being willing to allow others to be who they are, even if they are seemingly in the way of something you want. Allowing means understanding that the Universe allows everyone to have what they want, that there is no lack, that if someone has something you want, that you can have it as well, so it doesn't have to be taken away from someone else.

Allowing means understanding that another cannot be a part of your experience unless you invite them in through your vibration. The Law of Allowing means bringing your belief system into alignment with what you desire. It means not analyzing your beliefs and experiences to get there, it just means getting into a positive place.

23

The world is a very diverse place and there will always be something or someone that you don't want somewhere. And allowing means that those things or people must also be allowed by you. They must be alright with you. It truly means "letting go." It means your work is to get yourself feeling good anyway. It's about how you feel. And it is in this way that you attract joy and what you want.

Jesus, for example, used parables to explain this Universal Law. He said, "Turn the other cheek." He didn't mean, "Let them hit me again." He meant, "Allow them to be who they are. Turn your attention from that which you do not want, and give your attention to what you do want." He meant that you should simply *allow*.

I said this before, and it bears repeating again: this is one of the most difficult laws to manage. All the laws are of equal importance, but often what you want in life doesn't come to you as quickly as you would like because of this simple, yet involved, Law of Allowing.

Don't be hard on yourself. Actually, learn to smile at yourself as you learn to comprehend these laws, and use them the best that you can.

So, now, let's put these laws together and follow the process in this example. The steps to deliberate creating are:

Step One:
Ask. You are letting the Universe know what it is you want.

Step Two:
Source answers. This simply means that the Universe goes into action to fulfill your desire. It always hears you. This step is not your work. It just "is."

Step Three:
You let it in. This step is the allowing part, and that is your work; this is where you will expend most of your effort. You need to trust that the Universe will answer you, and that you will allow your creation in, by being a vibrational match to your desire.

And, so you say, "This is all too easy. If it's this easy, I should win the lottery, have everything I want, have the relationship of my dreams, have perfect children and a perfect job. Why don't I get everything good that I think of, or dream of, or have good feelings about?"

You have just asked the key question about being a deliberate creator, and in the next Chapter I'm going to address that important question. I wanted you to know the laws of the Universe, and now I want to take you to what makes them work, and why they sometimes don't "seem" to work.

It is as easy to create a castle as a button, and it is as satisfying to create a button as a castle, once you get the hang of all this.

Abraham-Hicks

 **Three**

The true cause of turbulence–
Delays in the Friendly Skies

There is magic in the Law of Attraction. It does not say that you are to ask and do all the right things and then it will be given. Instead, it is telling you to ask and not to offer contradictory thoughts to what you've asked for.

Thoughts from Linda

When you are clear in your wanting and asking, and you have lined your feelings up with your vibrations, you are ready for the Law of Allowing. But, it is here that you so often delay or delete the things that you have set into motion in the creative process. Please read these thoughts in that light.

In the creation process, there are often several things happening, and you can't always assign a delay to just one. There is a sense of "failure" that we humans love to hang on ourselves, so this sensitive area needs to be addressed before we proceed.

There is no "failure" and there should be no sense of despair over what you have manifested and where you are going. On this trip and adventure that we call "life," there is no right or wrong in the way that you have been culturally oriented to believe. There can be joy in contrast, and there can be joy and purpose in delays or change. There can be joy in not getting it right the first time, for the fun of getting it right later on.

This may sound too trite, but the truth is, the Universe is non-judgmental. The Universe is a loving energy that cheers you on every step of the way, never counting the steps it takes you to get to where you want to go. The loving Universe also understands that you never get it done.

It understands that sometimes you say you want one thing but you are vibrating another. It knows on the deepest levels what you want and sometimes delivers you a solution that seems like a surprise at first, but then you realize that it was your deeper desire. It is truly important to me that you read this information without judging yourself as you work with the processes.

The following topics are grouped together in this Chapter because they are often seen as reasons that good things don't happen. But they are also important to the creative process in a positive way. Nothing in your life or the Universe is mean-ingless. But–these are also a significant part of why you don't manifest your desires instantly!

Contrast
Contrast is much more than good and evil, right and wrong, or, black and white. Contrast is looking at the pros and the cons, the plusses and minuses, the yeas and the nays, without judgment or fear. It is an important step in creating. It assists you in identifying what you want. Without contrast, you do not move forward.

Contrast is one of those things you can't live without, and the creative process thrives on contrast. The difficulty with con-trast, though, is that you look at something not wanted, and you sometimes get stuck there, instead of seeing what you don't want and letting it inspire you to what you do want. And when you get stuck looking at negative contrast, you sometimes create exactly what you don't want because of the continued observation and emotion directed to the thing not wanted.

An example of how contrast works would be someone living in the heart of a major city and disliking the noise and crowds. Looking at that contrast without negativity (seeing what they don't want objectively) gives them the desire for what they do want (more suburban or rural living), and the desire for what is wanted becomes the focal point of a creation.

Used in another way, that same individual could be so focused on everything they don't want that they keep attracting the same thing, and they keep creating the unwanted environment. As a human, you are so oriented to believe that you should push against what you don't want, that this "pushing" has become a big part of your life. You have forgotten that this pushing against is interpreted by the Universe as vibration and wanting, and so you get exactly what you don't want, but feel strongly about. There is no such thing as "no" in this vibrational Universe…everything is "yes."

The real value of contrast is that it fine tunes your conclusions about something you really want. It often causes the passion that you need to feel to move your thoughts and feelings to the vibrational place you need to be at to create differently. 28

Each day you use contrast in both small and big ways, such as choosing your clothes or the color of your car by what you don't like.

The news media is observing and refining what you like and what you don't like. The news media is a constant source in your life for letting you see what you want and don't want. Contrast is everywhere in your creative decision-making world.

You can get caught up in your observation of contrast, in big and small ways. And then you think the laws of creation are not working for you, when in fact, they really are. You just have to remember to allow contrast to work for you in a positive way, to allow it to take you to what you really desire. *Contrast does not mean conflict. It simply "is."*

Resistance
Resistance is basically "negative emotion." I like to think of it as "stubborn negative emotion." It is also "pushing against."

How do you recognize resistance? Mostly you recognize resistance by how you feel. Anytime you are feeling bad, you are resisting what you are wanting. Resistance is definitely a disconnection to the Source of your creative energy. If you look at something and believe you can't have it or do it, you are resisting. Resistance could be identified by that tight feeling in your body. Sometimes it is something you have embraced for so long (a habit), that resistance feels almost like a normal feeling.

OK, you are already thinking that resistance is a bad thing. While it does get in the way of what you want, it is also linking you to your emotional guidance, just like contrast. And the next step to that is getting refocused on what you really want. Every emotion you have can be your friend when you learn to recognize the emotion and use it to get back on track.

Resistance is often linked to your belief system, whether it comes from you, your family, your culture or your society. We will cover this in the next few pages.

Your world and your life can be very dynamic and satisfying, if you will simply decide that you are going to contend with only your own vibrations; this is truly the path of least resistance. You've got to get resistance out of your vibration in order to have the revelation of that path to everything you want. You do that by reaching for the thought that feels good, not the one that feels bad...by reaching for the compliment, not the criticism...by reaching for the memory that thrills you, not the one that hurts you...by reaching for the positive aspect in someone, not the negative aspect.

The way you find your path of least resistance is by feeling your way. You can feel when resistance leaves and you can feel when resistance comes. You can feel when you're allowing, and you can feel when you're not allowing.

So, when you think about someone you want to love, who you feel negative towards and it's playing over in your mind how they should be different and you feel that knot in your stomach...stop and laugh and say, "This is not the path of least resistance and I am, for whatever reason, maybe even deliberately, choosing the path of more resistance, which certainly isn't good for me for a whole lot of reasons." Say to yourself, "I'm going to take the path of least resistance, and I'm going to find a positive aspect about that person."

At least you didn't keep driving forward on what was making you feel worse and you made an effort to pull back from that thought and you tried to find another thought. The path of least resistance is not a path of action. It's a mental path of allowing ease within your body right now.

Chapter Three Destination Joy

If you give yourself a little breath of fresh air by using the path of least resistance and do this again and again you will succeed in completely changing your thoughts and feelings...you will do a complete 180 degree turn. There is nothing that you have lived that you cannot lead yourself into the solution you are looking for.

Remember: when you change the way you feel...you change your point of attraction.

Dominant Thoughts and Beliefs
A dominant thought is just a well-practiced thought. It is a thought that you keep thinking. It is a habit. Dominant thoughts are very powerful and usually serve you well. Dominant thoughts stem from every source of your environment: your school, your church, your family, your culture, and events in your life.

It is when dominant thoughts are negative that they get in the way of your creative process. If you say, "I am always well, I just have a wonderful immune system," and you believe that, then you probably find sickness a rare event. Your dominant thought and feeling are serving you well. If you say (and believe) that, "All of my family is fat, and it's just our genetics, so I am fat," then you might have a terrible time with a diet until you find a way to adjust that dominant thought, to shift to a new thought that feels good.

What I want you to think about as we proceed in this section is: what are your most common feelings and thoughts during the day? What is the dominant feeling with everything you do? Everyone is different, but you are alike in that this dominant feeling creates the outcome for what you are wanting to create.

Your dominant feelings can be different for every subject that you encounter and everything you do. For example, you may have dominant feelings that serve you well with money, but dominant feelings about relationships that don't serve you well.

Awareness of your feelings helps with creating new dominant beliefs that serve what you want in a better way. I will cover shifting dominant thoughts (vibrations) as we proceed in the book.

Lack and Fear

Lack and fear rank near the top of the list of negative emotions that comprise dominant thoughts. These two emotions sabotage creative beings everywhere. I am giving them their own section because of their prevalence with us humans.

Lack

Lack is what occurs when you look at what you don't have and you get stuck in that "not having." It becomes a dominant thought over time, and then a habit. Sometimes lack comes from within your family and culture and you bring this lackful attitude with you from childhood to adulthood. *My family has never had enough money and I don't either.*

Lack is often inspired by the dominant thought that if someone else has something, there is not enough for me. The richest man in the world has so much money that there is not enough for the rest of us. Lack is not real. This is a bountiful Universe, but when you have been inspired to think that there is "not enough," then lack becomes a major roadblock to your creative desires, in whatever area you feel lack in.

Fear

I don't think I need to describe or define fear. Everyone knows the emotion and feeling of this thought. Fear is such a strong negative emotion, and it has delayed many creative wantings and desires. For example: fear of failure; fear of being worthy; fear that you might offend; fear that you aren't good enough; fear that you will say or do the wrong thing; and, fear that you won't get what you want; or, fear in any subject.

Fear is really disempowerment, because it saps your power by giving your attention to negative feelings and thoughts, which leads to creating what you do not want. In effect, your fear comes to fruition, and you make it real.

Negative Emotions

For the most part, this Chapter has been about negative emotions. They creep in, often unannounced and unwanted, or they are habits that you have yet to modify or shift. Call these emotions what you want: fear, lack, unworthiness, judging, blame, criticizing, guilt etc., etc., etc. Call them what you will. They are all the same thing. Negative emotion is negative emotion. All that negative emotions are, is disallowance from your connection to Source by giving your attention to what does not please you. And when you feel stuck in your negative emotions, you delay the joy and manifestations that you want. You are never really stuck; you just keep giving your attention to where you are, which keeps recreating more of the same.

Disallowing Energy

You can't disallow all of your energy, ever. But negative emotion creates a disallowance of some energy and distances you from the creative stream where Source is summoned and creation occurs.

Disallowing is the "pinching off" or "crimping" of the energy stream. No one does this intentionally, but negative emotion in all of its disguises delays what you are desiring. There are no compromises to your connection to Source. You are either allowing energy or you are not. What you may find amazing is that you can be allowing energy on one topic or event in your life but not allowing it in another simultaneously.

Let's look at this energy again. Everything is energy, and your attention to something means that it is in your energy in this moment, it is your point of attraction or how you are vibrating; this is true whether your point of attraction is vibrating negatively or positively.

The Universe is alive and pulsing with energy. It always has, and it always will. Every thought that has ever been thought, exists on an energy stream and is out there, pulsating with the Universe. As you stand in your moment, you perceive, intend, ponder, imagine, or think.

Whatever you are taking in during or at this moment–whatever you are giving your attention to–is causing you to offer a vibration. That vibration is giving you access to the past, present and future within the Universe–everything that is out there in the vibrational cosmos. (This is really a big thought, but it is so important that I want you to perceive your connection to the energy stream. It is cosmic and it is there for everyone. No one gets a bigger share. It is the unique gift of All That Is to give to you this creation ability.)

34

Always remember: you are a vibrational being. You are an electrical, electronic transmitter and receiver. You have an emotional guidance system within you to help you read that vibration. You are an extension of Source energy, and when you are truly allowing your electrical connection, you feel it and you feel *wonderful*. You feel passion, you feel eagerness, you feel empowered, and, you feel joy.

It is best described as a pure form of feeling, such as "feeling in love" all the time, or, as Abraham would say, "It's like liquid love." It is a state of no resistance and no negative emotion.

If you have desire that is focused and a habit of thought or a belief that doesn't quite match it, then you can feel the resistance from that. That's negative emotion. Negative emotion is what it feels like when you are summoning energy to create and you are not fully, vibrationally allowing that which you are summoning. In other words, negative emotion is not allowing your connection to Source energy.

Default

One last comment in this Chapter is on what prevents you from receiving what is promised in your deliberate creating. Sometimes people shut down their emotions, they stifle them, and they put a happy face on their negative emotions, and then try to stuff them inside. Sometimes you give up on thinking you will ever get the things that you are asking for and wanting.

The creative process doesn't stop when this happens. It goes on. But things begin to happen by "default." Default means having a vibration and not being aware that you have it. You stop making choices because negative emotion has made those choices seem painful, or you stop deliberately creating, for whatever reason, in certain areas of your life. In default, you are now creating without realizing what your role is in the process. It's a bit like being on remote, and feeling no control.

Default can also be giving your attention to things you don't want and creating them because you have not understood your place in the creative process. Default is what occurs when negative emotions have been with you for so long that you accept them as normal and don't realize the impact they're having on your creational direction.

Understanding and following through in the process of creating puts you back in charge. The Universe is loving, and it wants you in charge. The skies of the Universe are friendly, but delays happen to us all. We will discuss later how to work with this.

If you can create illness, you can create health.
If you can create poverty, you can create wealth.
If you can create failure, you can create success.

Abraham-Hicks

Chapter four

Appreciation and unconditional love–
Flying First Class

When you're in a mode of appreciation, your heart is singing. Then, you are joyful, and anything you can focus on is vibrationally accessible, because you are flowing your energy, and you are connected to your Source!

Abraham-Hicks

Appreciation: The most powerful tool for feeling good

Appreciation empowers you, while fear or other negative feelings are disempowering. And, you create what you want as a by-product of feeling good. This statement is so important, I find even the simplest terms don't explain the meaning of this as fully as I want you to understand it.

When you feel good, you are vibrationally in line with the energy of Source, and your energy is flowing in the most positive way possible. But when you are not feeling good, when you are experiencing any of the negative emotions, then the energy is pinched off.

As a simple beginning, you need to look for things to appreciate wherever you are and whatever you are doing. You can start in the morning with appreciating the bed you sleep in, your morning shower, the modern conveniences you rely on, the smiles on the faces of the people you see, the car you drive, and the road you drive on.

It's pretty easy to appreciate a sunny day or a beautiful flower or a smiling child. It is less easy to find things to appreciate in your car when it isn't responding; or when your boss at work is having a bad day and dumping on you; or when it's raining on your picnic; or when your checkbook isn't balancing; or when you are in the midst of a disagreement with a loved one. But, find something to appreciate in all of that anyway. As your appreciation grows–so do your rewards.

When you're in a mode of appreciation, your heart is singing. Then, you are joyful and anything you can focus on is vibrationally accessible, because you are flowing your energy, and you are connected to your Source!

As you begin to work with this powerful tool, you will see results that up until now have felt impossible. Appreciation is pure love, and it will change your life if you practice it, even once in a while.

As you begin to feel appreciation for the things around you, you begin to attract more things to appreciate. If the word "appreciation" doesn't feel comfortable to you, then use the word "love" or "gratitude" or any word that expresses well-being.

This might sound like a game, but when you let this enter into your life on a consistent basis, you will find that as your appreciation grows, your life flows. Appreciation is the purest, strongest form of unconditional love. Let's take that another step further: this is an important part of the creative process.

When you learn to appreciate what you already have and where you are now, then you will be on your way to achieving whatever you want next.

What keeps you from being in this loving, happy place? The opposite end of appreciating is a little negative word called "blame." Lots of people have somehow found it easier to judge, rationalize or blame rather than to appreciate. When interacting with people, it is easier to pick up on how they are projecting to you than how you are projecting to them. If you are dealing with angry or tired or upset people and they project their frustrations on to you, you tend to react and get defensive and jump right into their negative field. You tend to entrap yourself into someone else's thoughts and then get resentful and blameful in return.

Sometimes you have to appreciate a lot of negative people–finding something positive in them that you can appreciate. But the amazing part is that they begin to respond better to you. When you appreciate them quietly in your mind, relationships start to shift, or they go away.

When you expand the idea of appreciating within you, as you look for things to appreciate, you realize you are looking for reasons to feel good. And you will begin to notice that the more you appreciate, the better you feel about yourself and others.

Unconditional Love
Unconditional love means allowing love to flow through you. *39*
Unconditional love is really self-love because it is impossible to love someone else without reservation, without loving yourself first in that same way.

There is a myth that unconditional love is about loving others under impossible conditions and actions; that is not what I am speaking of here. I am speaking of the unconditional love of self that connects you to Source. You are not connected to Source when you are feeling bad.

Unconditional love says, "I want so much to feel good that I am going to find thoughts that connect me to Source energy, in spite of the conditions. If I am looking at something that makes me feel bad, I will withdraw my attention from that and find something, even if I have to find it in my imagination, that makes me feel good."

Unconditional love does not mean looking at negative things and loving them. Unconditional love means acknowledging, "I am a lover of life. My natural state is to feel good; therefore, I'm not going to demand conditions to be perfect for me to be in vibrational harmony. I'm going to stay connected to my Source because of my willingness to look at things that make my energy flow and feel positive." In other words, "I will not use the conditions (person, place or thing) to take me from my place of love within me, from my connection to Source energy."

In order to live your life joyously, you first have to really love and appreciate who you are. Were you instilled with a love of self as a young child? You were probably taught the reverse and taught that self-love was "selfish."

But, self-love is not selfish in the sense that you want everything for yourself. Self-love is about loving yourself enough to stay connected to your Source. And when you are connected to your Source, you can love outside of yourself. The way you feel about you is everything. When you adjust how you feel to feeling good without the condition changing, then you're on your way to joy.

Self-love is allowing love to flow through self. And love flowing through self feels like eagerness, passion, enthusiasm, and laughter. There are no more powerful tools in the Universe than "appreciation" and "unconditional love."

Chapter Four Destination Joy

 **five**

Health, wealth and relationships–
Frequent Flyers

When you change what you give your attention to, you change your point of attraction.

Thoughts from Linda

In my workshops, seminars and private sessions, the most frequently asked questions fall into what can almost be labeled "The Big Three." It is not surprising, since these are the questions of daily life.

These are the areas that concern us all: your *health*; enough *abundance* to provide you with the things you need and want; and, *people* to share your life with. While everything that can be said about these topics is directly related to the Universal Laws and your emotions, both positive and negative, it is important to address them separately.

Health
Your body is responsive to your thought. Everything is. The Law of Attraction applies to your body just as it does to other subjects.

You have not been trained in your physical life to know which thoughts or feelings represent the creative energy flowing. Without intending it, many people have turned the control of their bodies and their health over to others, letting them decide by observation, what health is, what is appropriate to eat or do for health, and how to care for the body when the observations suggest that all is not well.

42

You may select western medicine or alternative medicine or some other avenue for this information, but your culture has quite strongly set the stage for this to occur; actually, this is not a bad thing. The medicines and procedures and equipment and processes are very much a product of the desire of humanity to be well and to live long. The medical system satisfies mass consciousness. So, it is easy to believe that your health is controlled from outside of you rather than from within.

But, well-being truly does abound. And you really can control that once you understand that your life is about energies and vibrations. So, when you find the feeling place for wellness, everything responds to the vibration that you are sending out. When you actually achieve the feeling place about your health, everything about your wellness falls into place.

However, very few people in today's societies have achieved this kind of control over their health. You are bombarded with TV service announcements about every disease possible. Your TV shows and entertainment programming contain endless information about health. It is in your books, magazines and schools.

I would suggest, especially for the creative beginner, to begin to take control of health issues slowly. Shift your energies in small ways at the beginning. Appreciate the medical advances that are available to the public and utilize them when they feel appropriate to you. You cannot change deep rooted belief systems over night.

Consider modifying these beliefs thought by thought until you have the belief system of total well-being. Don't expect to do this in a short period of time.

You can try to avoid constant discussion of symptoms, illnesses, surgical procedures, etc. unless they point to wellness or well-being. Remember, it is possible to vibrate less than wellness through default, by attention to the subject, and an unintended focus. It all goes back to the Law of Attraction.

Begin to get a new view of your body and how you would like to feel, and let that be your focus. Want so much to feel good that you deliberately choose thoughts and actions that make you feel good about your body. You do have creative control over your body.

But be patient with yourself. I always recommend that you manage your body within the belief system that fits you best in the moment. Only you can decide what that means. It is your choice, and your body.

Wealth

It's not about money. It's about being in vibrational harmony with the well-being that you deserve.

Abraham-Hicks

Prosperity is a by-product of feeling joy. The way you allow dollars into your experience is by having desires that you are expressing positively.

44

Not having the financial abundance that you desire has all the same emotions around it that you find in other topics. You might feel a lack of money, that there is not enough to go around. You or a parent may have had a disappointment with money (stock markets, job loss) that creates fear or disappointment. You might not feel worthy of having much money, or you might be reacting in a negative way to the behavior of someone you thought used money inappropriately.

Whatever the root cause for the emotion, the solution lies within you and your ability to line your energy up with your desires. In addition to shifting your energy from negative thoughts and experiences, it is always important to visualize what you would do with the money you want as if you already had it.

Your awareness of your emotions is the first step in changing your vibration about prosperity. And then all the Laws of the Universe will come together for you. Ask. The Universe goes into action to bring you what you want, and your work is to get into the allowing mode to receive your requests. You do that by feeling good.

Abundance and prosperity are rampant on this planet; it's an abundant Universe. You just have to feel good from the inside and allow your abundance. Then, there would be very few questions on this topic. So, while you work with your desires and the Universal laws, be easy with yourself.

Relationships

You attract someone by means of your vibrations–so you attract whoever you are in vibrational harmony with. All of your relationships are a mirror image of your vibrations.
                                                            Abraham-Hicks

How you're feeling in every moment is what creates all of your relationships. You will be in a good relationship with others when you're in a good relationship with yourself (self-love and appreciation). But, when you're judging others, you are not defining them, you are defining yourself. It doesn't matter what another is doing, *how do you feel?*

If you define what you want more specifically, then you will draw those individuals to you who will enhance that. But if your intentions are not clear, you may attract what you don't want rather than what you do want. What you think and feel define the vibration that creates for you in your relationships.

Remember, *like attracts like*–that's the Law of Attraction. What are you focusing on, and how are you feeling?

You will discover true freedom when you discover that your joy does not depend on anyone else, and when you realize that *there are no victims.* Your joy only depends on what you choose to give your attention to, so set your own tone. Love yourself no matter what the conditions are; this is where unconditional love starts.

Everything in your life is about relationships. You have rela- tionships with your spouse, your family, your children, your friends, your co-workers and your supervisors, your romantic partners, your neighbors, the grocer down the street, your animals, even the traffic patterns you experience, and so on.

And, the greatest relationship you have is with yourself. When you nurture it, this relationship is one of self-love and self-appreciation. The result is that the energies and vibrations you emit provide a positive connection to your Source, you feel wonderful, and you create what you want in your life experience.

When you come from the love within you, the connection of your Source energy, you are not hurtable–because you're not coming from the love outside of you, you're coming from the love of your true self (unconditional love). Then you will have the most magnificent relationship you could want.

Remember, nothing is more important than your feeling good. It's that simple, because the Laws of the Universe determine your relational experiences based on your energies and vibrations.

What you are living today is a result of the thoughts and feelings that you have felt before this. Your future is created from your perspective of today.

Abraham-Hicks

 six

Energy flowing tools–
The Mechanics of Maintenance

Fantasize it; pretend it; remember things like it; visualize it, as if it already is; and, find the feeling place of it. Then, it WILL be there for you.

Abraham-Hicks

Staying in that good feeling place, in vibrational harmony, and living your joy–no matter what–is your life's work.

Again, *there is nothing more important than feeling good.* The tools and exercises I describe below are intended to assist you to get, and to maintain, the vibrational harmony you want. The by-product of setting your own positive vibrational tone is that you will create whatever you want to enhance your life.

There are many processes available to help you. I refer you, also, to Abraham-Hicks and their exercises on The Placemat Process, Virtual Reality, the Focus Wheel, Moving Up the Emotional Scale, and more.

In this guide, information is provided on the following:

1. Shifting Your Energy

2. Appreciation

3. Meditation

4. Creative Visualization

5. Scripting

6. Pre-Paving

7. Journaling

8. Positive Aspect Book

None of these tools and exercises is a magic key, but if any of them are helpful in assisting you to live your life joyously, then use them or modify them to suit your needs.

The two greatest tools are appreciation and meditation. If you went around appreciating all the time and only looked for the positive aspects–for thoughts and feelings that feel good–you would not need to meditate. You could just choose to meditate for that extra feeling of connection. OK, you could take 15-20 minutes per day to find things to appreciate (appreciation time or meditation time). Feeling good connects you to Source (i.e., aligns you to you). So, when you appreciate, you're in alignment, and when you meditate, you're in alignment.

Shifting Your Energy

When you are feeling any negative emotion, or you are giving your attention to something that you are not wanting, then moving away from this unwanted thing or emotion is called "shifting your energy."

The steps are:

1. Acknowledge the negative feeling.

2. Appreciate that negative feeling for showing you what you do not want.

3. Begin to talk yourself into a feel good place, thought by thought.

4. Continue with these positive statements until you find a place that feels good.

5. If you cannot reach a feel good place, then give your attention to another subject that feels good.

6. You can go back to the situation when you can approach it from a feel good place and see it the way you want it to be.

This process might sound like one that cannot be used in some situations, but you would be surprised how often it works in situations that are rather volatile. It is a mental "time out" accompanied by seeing the situation in a different light.

An example might be: you are at the airport and your flight is delayed. You have an important event at your destination, and you are feeling frustrated and not in control. Stop at this point and appreciate the feeling that your guidance system is providing. Your body and emotions are letting you know that you are not allowing your Source energy to flow.

Talk yourself through it thought by thought. Ask yourself, "What do I want? What are the results I want? How can I handle this in a way that feels good?" Reach for a thought and a feeling that feels good. Acknowledge the negative and shift it–thought by thought. Think and feel; think and feel.

Begin to look for statements that feel good. You might say, "I appreciate that they do not fly aircraft during severe weather. I appreciate that I am inside in a warm place to wait. I appreciate that I will arrive at my destination safely. I appreciate that I have some extra time for me. I appreciate that I live in a time that will allow me to get to my destination quickly. I appreciate the pilot. I appreciate the employees who are dealing with this situation." (You get the idea.)

If you cannot reach a feel good place with these statements, then give your attention to another subject. Think about the time you fell in love, or the wonderful vacation you had last year or some moment in time that feels good. When you can return to the subject, you will begin with more statements that ease your feelings about the situation.

Appreciation
The process of appreciation is a powerful tool. It is something you can do any time or any where–there are no boundaries. There are always things that you can find to appreciate; this is a tool to use all day, every day. Say, "I'm going to be an appreciator as much as I can." And then write your thoughts down and refer to them as often as you want. Remember, you appreciate because of who you are, not whether someone or something deserves it or not; just be the deliberate appreciator.

Appreciation Lists

List something or someone you're not happy with…and then list five positive things to appreciate about it or them. Begin to see them differently just from thinking about their positive aspects.

Write four or five new things each day that you can appreciate about yourself or your life.

You are appreciating yourself when you start saying "Nothing is more important than that I feel good." So, just go on a rampage of appreciation.

Abraham-Hicks

Meditation

Meditation is a good way to allow the energy.

Thoughts from Linda

What is meditation? Meditation is a tool that is used to lower your vibrational resistance. It is one of the greatest tools you have to enable you to connect more with who you truly are, your own inner Source.

Meditation is your most effective remedy: in meditation, your entire being dwells in a state of suspended time, which gives you the opportunity to be entirely in the present moment.

Meditation will move you beyond all external voices as well as beyond the boundaries of the physical senses. It will transport you into the Eternal Stillness–the Source of all creation. Meditation will assist you to allow your true self, and once there, you will be able to hear and feel your inner voice. It will tell you that you are loved and that you are magnificent, and that you are perfect–right now.

Meditation is akin to fine tuning a radio to a station that is broadcasting a beautiful symphony. But, most of the time, you may walk around tuned into nothing but static. The art of meditation precisely tunes your "dial" to the Source station so that you may hear the symphony–which provides music about your unity with Source. And, this does not end when the meditation is over. You bring more of this awareness back into your waking life. As a result, you become anchored in the awareness that you are your true self.

Meditation has been around for thousands of years. It's as old as time and as natural a process as breathing. Practitioners of this ancient art believe that regular meditation benefits both the mind and the body. It relaxes the brain into its most creative mode.

Meditation succeeds by narrowing your focus enough to quiet the barrage of signals your brain juggles every day. By doing so, your body feels relaxed and rejuvenated instead of being preoccupied, anxious, tense, angry or aggravated.

*Purpose of meditation...*The purpose of meditation is to clear negative thoughts, emotions, and resistance. When you meditate, you quiet your mind; when you quiet your mind, you stop thought, and you stop resistance. By stopping resistant thought, your vibration raises and you connect to who you truly are: your Inner Being, that spiritual, non-physical you. Just a few minutes of meditation each day can restore your tranquility and your sense of well-being, because you are shifting any negative thoughts or feelings and you are allowing your connection with Source to flow.

*Quieting the mind...*How does one close his or her mind to thought while meditating? There is no need to focus on quieting the mind entirely, just practice using the process. Every mind wanders. You become quiet enough in the process of meditation to gently focus back to your breath, or to thoughts of your Inner Being, or wherever you left off. The act of bringing your mind back is part of the meditation itself.

When you meditate, your goal is not to get carried away in thoughts that are not in vibrational harmony with your Source. Some teach you to hold a musical note, mentally or audibly, or to listen to the pounding of the surf, or the dripping of water, or other rhythmic sounds. The point is that you need to hold your thoughts in a vibration that has no lack, and these aids might help you to do that.

Meditation is difficult for some people because they have trained themselves to be responsive to their thoughts; then, trying to stop, or even slow down your thinking is not easy.

For example, rather than worry about quieting your mind at the beginning of your meditation, do just the reverse and let your mind go on a rampage of appreciation. Visualize something and find the good feeling that comes from it, and then gradually slow down your thoughts.

The real reason that quieting your mind is taught, though, is to give you the touchstone of well-being. You may have only a few moments of no thought, and that's fine, you're doing

54

OK. As you continue to practice meditation, just 15 minutes per day, you will experience more of the no thought, relatively quiet mind. Your goal is to stop resistance; then, you are in the state of allowing Source.

*Ways to meditate...*There are many teachers of meditation and many types of meditation and they all share a similarity. All types of meditation lead you to quiet your mind. I respect all of these varieties of common practices, but, personally, I like to keep the art of meditation very simple. There are also many techniques for achieving a meditative state, but one of my choices is to concentrate on the breath.

I meditate every morning, but you have to find the time in your day which is the proper time for you. You need to choose a comfortable time and a comfortable spot.

My special time of day is early morning when no one is up and it is still and quiet. I relax in a sitting position, shut my eyes and begin to focus solely upon my breathing, breathing slowly in and slowly out. If a thought interrupts my focus, I merely acknowledge it and return my focus to my breathing pattern.

There may be several interruptions by foreign thoughts, but each time I acknowledge them and immediately return my focus to my breathing pattern. If I have something that I want an answer to, or a question I have not been able to find an answer for, I will quietly ask my question of the Universe before I go into a meditative state and trust that the answer will come. Quite often, I will receive my answer either during my meditation or shortly after I have finished.

I usually allow about 15-20 minutes each day with this practice. In fact, if you can consistently do this each day for about 30 days you will notice wonderful experiences in your daily life.

Even though the breathing method is one of the ways I use, there are others which are just as satisfactory. Some people like to slowly count down from 100, focusing on each number. Others like to listen to the ticking of a clock or a timer. Still others use a mantra and repeat the same word or phrase over and over again. Use whatever method makes it easiest for you. In no manner should you make this difficult.

The power of the symbol that you use to aid meditation is that it should be something that has no negative attachment for you when you focus upon it. If you are focused upon something positive you have no room for thoughts of negativity, and your symbol will provide you a greater ability to concentrate and allow the energy to flow; that is why some feel that using positive symbols, mantras, and tones or sounds to help them meditate is beneficial.

Another meditation that I really enjoy doing is Mindfulness Meditation, which allows the thoughts to flow in and out like the tide, with no attention. It is going to the still, quiet place behind your thoughts.

*Meditation increases your joy...*When you meditate to strengthen the positive vibrational connection to your Source there are many benefits. There's a sense of overall well-being, and it's a wonderful way of being more in tune with your intuition, that sixth sense, allowing that broader part of you, that wise-being, to come through you. It's also a way of shutting down that inner dialogue–the judgment, the blame, the doubt, the criticism.

You know that deep within you, you have this place where you can clear the chatter. You go within for the silence and you connect to who you really are. It's sort of like your own secret place–your wise part. Your Inner Being is there and this is a way to connect with that God-force which is a part of you, your Source.

If you make a habit of meditating, your life will just flourish. You will have joy. You'll look at life in a more good feeling way, and you will feel more secure. You ask for what you want and you just listen for that inner voice.

When you meditate, your consciousness is withdrawing from that which you perceive in the moment. Sleeping is very akin to meditation, but there is a difference. In sleep, your consciousness withdraws but you are unaware of it, while in meditation you are *aware* of all that takes place. The greatest benefit of meditation is the feeling, or knowing, of the *oneness* with your connection with your Source energy.

All of your power is in your now. So, relax into your natural state of being–meditate–and feel your way to what you want.

Abraham-Hicks

Creative Visualization

Visualization is a good way to expand the energy.
Thoughts from Linda

The value of imaging... The value of imaging is so you can *see* something different–to get a new view that assists you in shifting your *feeling*. Most people are so busy doing what is immediate that they don't have the time, or they don't feel they have the time, to do what is really important.

If you could understand the leverage or the power in flowing energy, in imagery, in visualizing, you would spend 80% of your time doing that and 20% of your time doing whatever else you do.

Really, you would be better off spending 20% of your time in action now and spending 80% of your time in day-dreaming and doodling in notebooks and planning what it is you want. Before you can do that with ease, though, you have to understand the Law of Attraction–you have to trust that the Universe is helping you.

My encouragement to you is to just *act less and image a little more.*

Role-play a few things, focus on something for a few seconds and find a good feeling place about it and then watch how quickly the Universe brings you something about your subject. Then do it again with something else and watch how quickly the Universe brings you something about that. It's best to start with subjects or things that you have no resistance to.

Continue this until you've proved to yourself that the Universe is aware of you and is responsive to you. Once you've got those two things figured out, then it's up to you how much you want.

If you give yourself the opportunity to focus on anything long enough by feeling good, to let the Law of Attraction take hold of it, passion will ultimately be the result of that. There are all kinds of things that are waiting in the wings, that once your thoughts hook into it, it may very well be the thing that opens the door for you. And the more fun it is, the more likely it will be to do that.

See it–believe it–feel it–and it will happen. Begin the magic now…

Thoughts from Linda

*Creating with your imagination…*Imaging is just using your imagination to see and feel something that is not yet there. Imagination means taking an image and adding power to it. So, when you take an image and you focus your creative attention upon it and hold yourself in vibrational harmony with that image, you and the image are vibrating the same, and the Universe will find things that match it, to bring them to you.

Visualization, imagining, or imaging is the most important factor in the creative process. Only by seeing them the way that you want things to be can the Universe bring them to you. This feeling (of allowing) is what creates the vibrational harmony with the object, and the vibrational match brings (attracts) it to you.

Worry, on the other hand, is using your imagination to miscreate. In other words, you are creating by default. So become consciously aware of your emotions. Understand what your emotions are telling you. Withdraw from any habit of observing what is, and begin to use your power of imagination more.

Think about what the word imagination implies…image-a-nation…it's limitless.

Holding an Image:

Means…
I'm holding a vision, and I'm creating a vibration, that by the Law of Attraction,

Is this thing that…I'm imaging, I'm vibrating, I'm projecting, and the Law of Attraction is matching.
Abraham-Hicks

Use the power of your imagination and create any reality that you choose. But as this reality is unfolding, know that it is only the jumping off part; it's a jumping off point for the next image.

Act much less and imagine much more.

*Creative visualization process…*The progress of change does not occur on superficial levels, through mere "positive thinking." It involves exploring, discovering, and changing your deepest, most basic attitudes towards life. That is why learning to use creative visualization regularly can become a process of deep and meaningful growth.

60

In this process you often discover ways in which you have been holding yourself back, blocking yourself from achieving satisfaction and fulfillment in life through your fears and negative concepts. Once seen clearly, these limiting attitudes can be dissolved through the creative visualization process, leaving space for you to find and live your natural state of happiness, fulfillment and love.

At first, you may practice creative visualization at specific times and for specific goals. As you get more in the habit of using it, and begin to trust the results it can bring you, you will find that it becomes an integral part of your thinking process. It becomes a continuous awareness, a state of consciousness in which you know that you are the constant creator of your life.

Your work is to: dream it–image it–feel it...and let it happen.

Abraham-Hicks

Just remember to visualize with pure thought, no negative after-thought, and stay with your visualization just as long as you continue to feel good. This kind of exercise is really "creating your virtual reality" that I talked about above, and you are doing it by these steps: "Get In–Feel Good–Get Out."

It's really that simple, because the purpose of creative visualization, imagination, imaging, or a virtual reality exercise is to create vibrational harmony with whatever you want, and let it come to you.

Think it; image it (mental vision); feel it as if it is; and hold the vision...trust the process.

Thoughts from Linda

Scripting

*Scripting to focus your attention...*Scripting is a process in which you tell the Universe the way you want something to be as if it already is, and get into the feeling place of your story. It's the best process if you have something that you want that has yet to come to fruition, because scripting can speed it up. It is literally breaking the habit of telling everybody how it is now, and beginning a new habit of telling everybody how you want it to be.

Scripting is a sort of heavy-duty re-orienting by offering your vibrations deliberately through specific words. It is pretending, like you are a screenwriter, wherein you get to decide the characters, and you get to weave them together in a scenario that pleases you.

*The process of scripting...*You can begin by portraying yourself as the central character and name the other main characters in your scenario, and then just begin plotting the story out. It is most effective if you write it, especially in the beginning, because writing is your most powerful point of focus.

But, once you've written it a time or two, each time you write, enhance it a little bit. Then you reach the point where you can just mull it over in your mind, until eventually you begin to vibrate as if it is manifesting now. If you feel your script often enough, you accept it as reality, and the Universe believes it and responds in the same way.

Pre-Paving

*Pre-paving (or pre-planning) how you want something to be...*Pre-paving is deliberately thinking through writing or talking through the details of a situation or circumstance in advance, to help you envision and feel how it's going to be.

Pre-paving is a way that you set the tone of your energy more deliberately. As you begin to develop the habit, you will begin to notice that your life is moving along a lot smoother–because you have pre-planned it.

Journaling

Why keep a journal? People keep journals for many reasons, but one reason to write in a journal is so that you can *reinforce your thinking and feeling* to create vibrational harmony with what you want. The act of writing it all down trains you to think along those lines. If you keep a journal, remember to write from a positive place.

When you have taken the time to envision something, to pre-pave it and even to write it down, so that the energy of the Universe has preceded you, then you are *inspired* to the place you want to be. As you imagine something, and write about it, what you've imagined exists. It begins to pulse and literally will draw you to it. That's what impulses and inspirations are.

So, the rule of thumb is, "The more you have felt it, visualized it, and scripted it, and written or talked about it, the more you've become a vibrational match to the results as you want them to be, and then the more you will be vibrationally in a place for that feeling of inspiration."

Positive Aspect Book

*Create a positive aspect book...*Here is another journal type of exercise: creating a "positive aspect book." A positive aspect book is a book that records the things you are looking at in a positive way.

Here is how it works: Take a notebook, and call it your "Book of Positive Aspects (per Abraham-Hicks)." Spend ten minutes each day writing positive aspects about your home, your body, your work, and your relationships. When you wake up every morning, acknowledge that you have re-emerged into the physical from your sleep, and that today you will look for more reasons to feel good. And, if you pay attention to the way that you are feeling, within 30 days you will see such a dramatic turn of events in your life experience, that you will not believe that you are the same person.

Here are some positive statements that you can write if you want to be a success:
"I am successful."
"I am proud of what I do."
"I can figure anything out as I go along."
"I have the resources to get anything into place
   that I need to."
"I am resilient."
"I am professional."
"I am honest."
"I have your best interest at heart."
"I am really good at what I do."
"I have far more capacity than I have ever begun to tap into."
"I would love it if you would stretch me and pull
   more from me."
"I am up and ready to perform that."

64

All of these statements are a match to who you are, and once you project something like this, the Universe responds to it.

Journaling exercise for deliberate creation... Another journaling exercise is to focus on specific desires and write about them to bring them closer to your reality. In the beginning, target three or four of your primary desires. Eventually, you will be able to simultaneously create in unlimited directions, but as you are learning the process, it is best to focus in only three or four directions.

Select those desires, wants or intentions that are most important to you in this time and write each of them at the top of a sheet of paper in this way: "I intend to receive..." and write whatever it is that you are intending to receive. Then, take each of those sheets of paper, individually, and complete them, one at a time, as follows: below your statement of intent, write: "These are the reasons that I intend to receive..." and then restate your intention. And write all of the reasons that you want this.

Chapter Summary
Make your lists of things that make you *feel good*. Use any process or exercise or tool that assists you to feel good. Gather your musical tapes that make you feel good. Eat in the restaurants that make you feel good. Interact with your friends that make you feel good. Reminisce about those memories that make you feel good. Fantasize those visions that make you feel good. Attend those workshops that make you feel good. And watch those television shows that make you feel good. Do anything that makes you feel good.

Revisit everything that makes you feel good. And when you're not watching what you're doing, and you bump up against something that doesn't feel good, release yourself from it, don't condemn it, just allow it to be, and accept that it exists, then turn and look at something that is more compatible with your natural state of being. Look at something that feels good. Look for all reasons to feel good.

Just remember, there are only two emotions: feeling good and feeling bad. When you feel good you are connected to your Inner Being (Source), and you feel joy and love; but when you are feeling bad, you are in some sense disconnected from your Inner Being, and you are feeling lack, or fear.

In every moment of every day, look for things to appreciate. You always have a choice as to what you want to give your attention to. Ask yourself, "What have I denied myself, and for what reason?" If you're not creating something you want, it's because you're not allowing it in, and it's because of your resistance, or some negative feelings.

Your mantra is, "What I think, what I see and what I feel will be what I'm going to get!" Remember, the Universe doesn't know when you're offering a vibration if it is being offered because you're living it or because you're imagining it. The Universe doesn't know what is real and what is imagined, and it doesn't ask for your resume…it just takes you at your now vibration and responds to it.

Also remember, nothing is more important than that you feel good, that you feel your joy. So, wherever you go, or whatever you do, look for reasons to feel good. In doing so, you allow your connection to Source energy, and nothing is impossible.

Clean out the clutter…mentally and physically…and laugh your way to success! Laughing is the physical embodiment of pure, positive energy. It's the sound of your Inner Being coming forth from the non-physical.

Thoughts from Linda

 seven

Putting it all together–
A Joyful Journey

These are the steps in the path of creating:

1. You create in your life by how you *think and feel* because this is a vibrational Universe, and that is how your energies flow. You are *guided* in your creating through your emotions, by the pure, positive non-physical energy (your Inner Being). When you listen to your inner guidance (when you're in harmony with it), it's taking you forward.

2. Your path follows three very powerful laws of the Universe: the Law of Attraction, the Law of Deliberate Creation, and the Law of Allowing. You are always creating, so you are either a deliberate creator or you create by default.

3. You create what you want as a by-product of feeling good. You are in vibrational harmony with your Inner Being when you feel good; that is why your quest is to *seek joy* in your life. Finally, you will achieve joy by *appreciating* yourself and all things.

4. So, when you are feeling good, you are *allowing the connection* of who you really are to flow here and now, and that's what matters; this is what your life is really about.

68

How do you make this work?

It is always much easier to talk about how this works than it is to put it into practice. But practice is just what it takes, along with a sense of humor and the continued awareness that you never really get this creation stuff done.

In my workshops, it is easier to work with specific examples brought up by workshop participants than to give a written example. When we talk a problem through, with the give and take, it is easier to follow than a transcript.

However, I want you to follow the sequence of what happens in a real situation, but I also want you to follow it without too much emotional intensity (and therefore possible resistance) until you get a feel for the process. So, I am intentionally picking an example that won't have a lot of emotional entanglements for you. I'm staying away from health, wealth and relationships for those reasons!

Let's stay with our travel theme, just for fun:

You have been asked to plan a dream trip for you and nine of your friends. You have been asked to pick the destination and activities. They haven't given you much input on where to go or how much to spend, but you do know about how long they can be away from their jobs. And you know them rather well in terms of travel likes and dislikes.

You go through travel books, the Internet, and talk to travel and tour agencies, seeking all kinds of information and advice. In a short period of time, you are getting very excited and enthusiastic. You are very focused on this task and you are putting a lot of energy into your effort.

Law of Attraction has brought you and your friends together. You are pretty much like-minded and enjoy each other's company. As a group, you appear diverse, but the common threads that make you a group of friends seem obvious to you most of the time.

The Law of Deliberate Creation is evidenced by your attention to the project, their wanting you to do the project, and the feelings each of you are holding deliberately.

You recall that there are three steps to the creative process: *You ask* (you want to have a great trip), *the Universe responds* (you can't see this, but when you ask, the Universe brings what you want to your doorstep.) And then, the final step is *allowing* what you are asking for. It is here, as we have discussed, that you often get into trouble; this is the place where you tend to get in your own way.

Let's look at it as we continue in our example. After careful consideration, you decide to propose a safari to an exotic resort in Africa. You gather your friends together, and with great enthusiasm, you present your plan. You are very excited, and you can see you and your friends having a wonderful time. You have no resistance to this destination and adventure. In your mind, you are there!!!!

70

What happens next is what happens in life. You begin to observe, react and "hook" into the observations of others.

You get "moved off the track" by others' opinions, and you move those things into your vibration. You were vibrating purely with this project and then, when it was presented, your friends began to find fault with what you proposed.

Friend One said, "They have so many problems in Africa with disease and unrest, so will we be safe?" Friend Two said, "I hear you have to get shots in advance. I don't like the idea of that, nor do I like taking medications that I understand are required or advised." Friend Three said, "That's too long a flight." And, Friend Four chimed in with lots of opinions about the cost, and asked, "If you have to go to the better resort, could you cut corners and save money?" Fortunately, your other friends were as enthusiastic as you with your plan, but the group began to "sink" with the observations and opinions of the four.

You feel yourself begin to feel unappreciated for all the time you have spent on this project. They could have given you some input or help if they were going to be resistant. And your mind begins to chatter with all the little thoughts that come when you are confronted with differing opinions.

It is here that you have to remember that you are a creator for yourself, but that you can't create in other peoples' experience. You can allow their opinions, but should not get caught up in them. You have to focus on feeling good first. That doesn't mean getting your own way: that means feeling good no matter what others say or think or do. It isn't necessary to push against your friends to have what you want.

So, it is here that you would shift your energy to remain

happy about what you are planning and proposing. You would allow the others to have their feelings and opinions, without pulling those ideas into your reality. Get back into your good feeling place and keep your excitement. Appreciate the guidance system within you that lets you feel anxious, a little annoyed, clearly not in vibration with what you were wanting.

You were wanting everyone to be as excited as you, and approving of your suggestions. It didn't happen, but your emotional guidance system, by showing you that anxiety feeling, was how you knew you were getting off track from what you wanted.

To Friend One, you would appreciate him and allow him to discuss his fear. If he can't talk himself into a better position, then appreciate that it might be better for him not to participate in this experience; that doesn't prevent you or others from doing so. To Friends Two, Three and Four, you would do the same. The important thing here is not getting into their vibrations and negative energy, if that is the stand they are taking. You don't have to join them. If you push against them, and disagree with them, you have actually joined them in their resistant, negative place.

Many of the processes we discussed in Chapter Six could be used here to make you feel better. Most of them work best when you are not in the middle of the situation causing you discomfort or removal from your good vibration. That is OK. Most of life's creative situations don't require you to take immediate action. And there is no right or wrong, because the creative process is continuous.

If you reacted to your friends with annoyance, then be gentle with yourself. You can always shift it to a better feeling place. You often get so caught up in the opinions and observations of others that you vibrate with them and often don't get what you want as quickly as you would like.

All of the processes we discussed could be used here, if time permitted. I can't say it enough. The important thing in all of life's situations is that you find a way to feel good inside. It may not come immediately, but you can move towards feeling good in small steps.

You can go in several directions with this scenario. You could all get angry and never speak to each other again. That probably wouldn't feel good, but it is a possibility. You could acknowledge that the fears and concerns of your friends are real to them and allow them to not participate in the trip without judging them, or you could give them time to think their concerns through.

Let's say the group decided to meet again in a week. At that time, two of the resistant friends had gotten information that made them feel better about the trip. Two of them didn't. So, eight of you decided to go on the trip, loving your two friends who decided not to go, for their right to make that choice. In the week in between, you found occasion to use most of the processes we discussed in Chapter Six to help you remain vibrationally in tune with who you are and what it is that you want.

You will "put it together" in the creative process all of your life. Have fun with it; this is life. Life isn't about getting stuff (even though you will!), it's about being happy and joyful as you live each day, allowing your connection to Source.

Your work is to feel as good as you can, about as many things as you can. Say, "I want, therefore it is."

Chapter eight

Happy landings

Nothing is more exhilarating than to dance through life recognizing the Universe is there to yield to you whatever you want, whenever you want it.

Abraham-Hicks

Life is your workshop.....Life is a workshop where you can, on a daily basis, fine-tune all aspects of your life. You have the ability to create the kind of life you want and to become the person you really are. Everyone is different from the next person, and yet, when you bring all of your uniquely different perspectives together, tremendous motion forward is achieved.

We've said that everything is energy, and your life is about the flow of that energy. It's all about energy. It's all about vibrations. You are an extension of the energy that originally created the earth, and you vibrate that energy constantly; that energy flows through everything on this earth. You are an electronic field of this energy, and so you are like an electrical transmitter and receiver.

This energy is the Source energy, the God-force or Universal energy or All That Is. You were that non-physical, spiritual energy before you came upon this earth, and once here you became a blend of both non-physical and the physical. When you choose to leave the physical form you are still the non-physical energy as that is who you truly are, whether you are in-body or out-of-body.

I've shared that how you feel is how you will vibrate and flow your energy; therefore, what you vibrate is what you create in your life. Your creations reflect the way you are vibrating at all times. *Remember, how you feel about you is everything.* It is the powerful Law of Attraction that brings it all together accurately and perfectly.

In simple terms, if you are feeling good, you are allowing the energy to flow through you, and if you are feeling less than good you are blocking the energy flow and manifesting less than you desire. *And, when you shift your feeling to feeling good without the condition changing, then you have changed your point of attraction.* So, it is through your feelings that you either allow or disallow the things you wish for throughout your life.

Finding Your Joy: Peace and Passion
What is the difference between "peace" and "passion"? Passion is extreme, compelling emotion. It is heartfelt excitement, enthusiasm, and a fondness for something. It is also clear, undiluted energy; having no resistance. Passion occurs when you focus on your desire for what you want, and you do not water it down!

What do you feel passionate about? Ask yourself...Is my Inner Being joining me in this thought or am I just banging around on my own? Your passion lets the energy flow to you in a pure, positive way. It is: having no resistance.

Abraham discusses the differences among "joy," "peace" and "passion." Joy and passion have the same vibration. Both joy and passion are undiluted energy, as I have said. When most people use the word "passion," though, they are thinking of the personality trait of "excitement," and the contrast of the low emotion when there is no excitement. The observable high looks like passion to some people, but it's really excitement.

Some people do have noticeable highs and lows. These emotions look like passion to some people, but more laid back people are not short on passion either. They just appear to be peaceful, or in harmony with themselves and others, or contented; in other words, they do act out the non-physical energies of who they truly are. "Peace" is often seen as a low-key or neutral zone.

Someone once asked me about passion. For example, I feel good all the time, yet I'm not a visibly emotional person. I just want to feel "joy," which is my contrast to "passionate joy." I feel that I have passion, but I don't have the personality trait of excitement that others might see from the outside as excitement and interpret as passion. But, I really feel a passion from the inside that is like a glorious, flowing feeling bursting forth from within me.

Real passion, then, is that clear, non-contradicted energy flowing through you. You know it when you feel it. It's joyful. And, it cannot be diagnosed from the outside since it is something that you feel from the inside.

Ultimately, if you use contrast incrementally, so that you continue to open up more and more, you will not have great highs and lows, but you will be on an even keel of feeling joy, and peace, and harmony all the time; that's why your life is about a constant process of refining your feelings. Over time, or with practice, you will not have great swings of highs and lows, but steady, continuous joy.

On your journey to "joy"...How can a person generate energy? There are two ways to rev up the energy.

The first is to let contrast help you do it. Suppose you are in an uncomfortable situation, one that is not all that heavy but does bother you a bit. If you think about it and analyze it and talk about it over and over it is certain to become larger and larger until it really becomes a major hurdle. When you realize how large it has become you can say, "Hey, this isn't what I want. Instead, I want this…" So, the contrast will sort of prod you into a decision.

The other way to rev up energy is to parlay a positive thought into a larger, more positive thought. You don't have to go where you don't want to be, to get where you do want to be. You can go from where you are toward where you want to be to accomplish more of the good stuff.

So, if you look at your life and you are content with where you are and what you have, that is peaceful appreciation. You're not asking the energy to come forth and change things. If you are focused upon something general, it usually feels more peaceful and contented.

If you say, "I want to develop an empire where I can be a financial mogul that generates great income, for thousands of people to benefit by my enterprise," that statement is more specific, or more passionate. Of course, the contrast of "I don't yet have that empire..." can set up negative emotions. So, appreciate where you stand, as you focus on where you want to be, and give that your passion.

You have to work on building that more specific, more passionate vibration, by working at producing sixty-eight seconds of positive vibrations to actualize your ideas, in increments of seventeen seconds at a time. If you stay with the subject just a little longer, the ideas begin to attract others and grow. Anytime you stay with a subject, it will grow. It has to, because this is how the Law of Attraction works.

A Simple Formula for Living...Abraham-Hicks
• Every day, look for things to appreciate. And then...

• Make written lists of tangible things around you to appreciate.

• Start a personal campaign to find the positive aspects of anything and everything you are giving your attention to. And, in doing that, you will automatically be aware of your guidance system, so that you will catch yourself, if ever you are doing the opposite of that.

• Pay more attention to the way you feel. And when you find yourself feeling positive energy, stop and say, "Ah! I am, right now, achieving vibrational harmony with something I want." And, then, do more of it.

- If you were to find yourself feeling negative emotion, you would stop and say, "Ah! My guidance system is working. I can feel that I'm looking in the opposite direction of something I want." Then, pat yourself on the back for acknowledging that you are flowing energy. Identify what you would prefer instead, and find that feeling place, and then continue to do more of that.

- Bask more. Spend more of your time thinking about what you want and less of your time trying to do anything about it.

- Every day, make a list of how you want to feel. Then, make a list of things to do. If, by habit, you make a list of things to do first, then, go back, and make a list of how you want to feel relative to the list of *things to do*.

- Your focus is joy. And when you focus upon your desire for *joy*, you connect yourself with your guidance, which lets you know how you're flowing. And, when you're connected to your guidance, *growth* is assured.

- Trust that "all is well," and in knowing that, you will release your tension that is keeping the well-being from you, right here and now.

- For the most part, you are a being who is acknowledging that you are a deliberate creator. Don't make big work of all this. Relax and have fun.

- Nothing is broken or needs to be fixed. Your work is to relax and enjoy your journey more.

- If anybody asks you what you do for a living, tell them that you collect data. Tell them that you examine the data of the Universe and as you do so, you decide what feels best. And then, give as much of your attention to that as you can, and the Universe will give you more of it. Tell them that you are spiraling upward and that things are getting better and better.

- When somebody says to you, "How are you?" say to them, "Great! And, I don't know why. I guess I must just deserve it."

- When somebody says, "How is it that things are going so well for you?" say, "I can't explain it, but well-being just seems to abound." Tell them, "The same energy that makes the sun come up every morning and keeps my heart pumping even while I'm sleeping, seems to be the same grace I'm living with every day."

- "People are nice wherever I go, and in my travels, the traffic just flows. All is very well in my world." And, they will say, "My God, where do you live?"

- You will say to them, "I live where you live, I just vibrate in the knowing that all is really well." And, little by little, they will join you.

- Remember, your work is not to fix it for anyone. You teach by your example. Your work is to connect to the energy and let it flow through you, and everything will fall into its perfect order.

*Reaching for your magnificent life...*If you want a magnificent life you have to begin to say, "What type of magnificent life do I seek? What sort of life would that be?" If what you're living now IS a magnificent life, then give it all the attention, all the appreciation and all the focus you can give, saying, " I want more of this, more of this, more of this." If you have something that makes you feel good, say, "I appreciate and want more of this."

Alternately, if you have things that do not make you feel good, appreciate them and go back to that which makes you feel good. Never dwell on that which makes you feel bad, Just talk yourself through it and shift your thoughts and feelings to that which makes you feel good.

If the life you really choose is one of magnificence, then you have to visualize it as being magnificent. You have to see yourself as having the things you want, and doing the things you would like to do, and being the way you would like to be.

Imagine it, fantasize it, pretend it, do anything you have to do to get the feeling of how you want things to be. Imagine that you're already at that destination; imagine that you're living your life as you'd like it to be.

When those negative feelings come to the surface, and on many occasions, they will, acknowledge them, appreciate them for showing you how you don't want to feel, and then shift them into feelings that make you feel better, on the way to your destination.

Shift those feelings to ones of happiness, wellness, bliss, of making good choices, of having more purpose, of having fun and making it easy for yourself, of being able to allow, of freedom and worthiness, give yourself approval, bask in the glory of things, be deliberate in all of your creations. Just feel good.

To live that spiritual, physical well-being, all-is-well, magnificent life–give your attention to what you want, appreciate where you presently are, feel good and feel joy in the moment. Make it simple.

Recipe for Eternal Joy:

- Seek joy...first and foremost.
- Seek reasons to laugh.
- Seek reasons to offer words of praise–to self and others.
- Seek beauty in nature, beasts, and other humans.
- Seek reasons to love. In other words...in every segment of every day...look for something that brings forth within you a feeling of love.
- Seek that which uplifts you.
- Seek opportunities for offering that which uplifts another.
- Seek a feeling of well-being.
- Know that your value can only be measured in terms of joy.
- Acknowledge your absolute freedom to do any of these things or to not do any of these things–for it is, without exception, your choice in every moment of every day.

Abraham-Hicks

93

This is the recipe for eternal joy. And it will also provide a format for a life of dramatic, magnificent creating. This may feel like the "bottom line" to you: "How much success, or how much acclaim…how much value can I offer here and now?" Just remember that your value can only be measured in terms of *joy*.

Once you get upon that path where you are seeking and finding, you are abundant with joy. The nice thing about this is that you cannot seek something without finding it. It cannot be. For that which you are asking for is always that which is coming to you. Ask and you shall receive. Let every day be a holiday, a celebration of joy!

The main event is the joy you feel. Are you observing it or are you creating it? It is the way you feel that is important. When you are looking at the flaws in the world, it is not about the world, it is about you. It is about the way you feel about you. Nothing is more important than establishing your own relationship with you.

Your road to your magnificent life…Everyone has the potential to change their life. Within each person's grasp is a rich life which is influenced by the choices you make. Every thought, emotion, feeling, attitude, action and belief affects the outcome of that life which you ultimately live.

Just remember, it's not what you do and think that creates the results, it's how you feel about what you do and think that creates the results.

You can feel good about the flower you're looking at...the ocean you're gazing across...the smile on a happy child's face or the good feeling you achieve just by petting your pet. If you can be focused upon something like that, and feeling utter well-being, then, in that moment of basking, you are attracting the dollars you want, the relationship you want, or the abundance of all things that you want. You are attracting whatever it is that you truly desire. You see, it's always about vibrating and allowing.

You don't have to work at your high vibration. Your higher, purer vibration is natural to you. But, you do have to let go of the thoughts and feelings that are holding your vibration down! The better you feel, the more you are allowing, and you are staying on the road you want to be on.

Happy landing, my friend. I wish you a joyful journey in your magnificent life.

The way you become a creative force, utilizing energy, is by your perspective, by your belief, by your attention, by your focus, by your decision. The next creation will be a direct response to the last vibration you activated.

Thoughts from Linda

Addendum

Thoughts from Linda

This selection of "Thoughts from Linda" was e-mailed to those on her mailing list on the dates listed below. If you are interested in receiving future "Thoughts from Linda" on a bi-weekly basis, please contact her at: lindafallucca@ameritech.net. You may also access Linda's website at: www.lindafallucca.com for upcoming events.

May 13, 2004
LIFE'S JOURNEY

Creation is about relaxing and releasing the resistance, which is the only thing that is keeping you from anything that you want. Creation of anything, or the distance from where you are to any place you want to go, is an emotional distance.

If you don't have enough money and you want more money, you probably think that the journey is from "not enough money" to "more money." You think that the journey is to find a way to get more money, but the journey is to find a way of not feeling bad about not having enough money. The journey is to find a way of not feeling bad about where you are.

The journey is about finding relief because, when you are able to feel around somewhere and find some thought that gives you a little relief, no matter what it is, and it may not be a thought that anybody else thinks (it doesn't matter how anyone else thinks about it), if it gives you a feeling of relief, you've released some resistance. And, when you release some resistance, now the world opens to you in another way for creating.

So, creation is really more about loving yourself...it's more about feeling your worthiness, appreciating you, appreciating a friend, enjoying the sunset and enjoying the beautiful flowers...it's more about finding reasons to relax into well-being rather than pushing against what you do not want...because you are to be the receiver of the love and well-being that is you.

In other words, there is no limit to how good you can feel and what you can create. Every thought is the journey, your emotions are your guidance system—so think and feel—look for the thought that feels good in every situation...

Feel the joy, feel the appreciation, feel the eagerness, and let your contrast be from feeling good, to feeling joy, to feeling passion.

April 29, 2004
WHAT IS NORMAL...

Most of our waking moments, we're functioning behind a mask...living a functional, but passionless, life. We are so used to thinking and feeling negative thoughts, and standing in judgment or justification, that we think this is normal. Believe me, it is not normal.

When we become aware of how we feel, in each and every situation, knowing that we have a choice in how we feel, we can acknowledge the negative feeling and then shift, thought by thought, to one of feeling good...knowing that we create our own lives by how we think and how we feel.

We can feel our own power, our own clarity, feel and allow our full connection and feel as though we can not only fly, but soar. We can become one who easily appreciates...one who loves whatever we do in the moment and one who loves every part of life and creates a passionate and joyous life experience.

Then we can remove that mask and allow the loving, magical powerful being we truly are, to just be.

April 15, 2004
YOU ARE THE CREATOR OF YOUR LIFE

I'm sitting here recalling a story I heard, about a wise Sage who lived in a very small village. He was the one man everyone came to for solutions and guidance. There was a small group in the village that decided they would try to fool, or trick, the wise Sage.

Their method was to catch a bird and one member of the group would hold the bird in his hand and hold his hand behind his back and then would ask the wise Sage, "Is the bird I hold in my hand dead or alive?" If the wise Sage answered that the bird was alive, the man holding it would squeeze the life out of the poor bird. If the wise Sage said that the bird was dead, the man would just set it free.

The group knocked on the wise Sage's door and when he answered, one of the group asked him, "Is the bird I hold in my hands dead or alive?" The wise Sage answered, "The life you hold is in your hands."

This reminds me that the life we experience is the one we create...one we hold in our hands. It is all manifested by how we think and how we feel. You cannot find a solution when you're looking at the problem, as then you are vibrating with the problem, and when you are vibrating with the problem, you're resistant to the solution.

Reach for the feeling that feels best in order to create the solutions, as you live your lives with joy.

April 1, 2004
APPRECIATION

No matter who or what you may be having a problem with, you have the ability to shift your own vibration. All you have to do is access the Source energy that is within you and radiates from you, by getting a thought that makes you feel good...by observing and appreciating more of the wonderful things life has to offer.

Instead of analyzing and agonizing over difficulties, just look for things to appreciate. In this way you'll begin to experience a happier life, ever more.

You really don't have to completely understand "energy flow" or "vibrational dynamics"...if you will just make a habit of looking for things to appreciate, it will be the only tool you will ever need to enable the energy to flow. Make a game out of this: practice, practice, practice feeling the emotions you want to emit. Practice, practice, practice appreciating and allowing. Practice feeling good. Do your very best to release any negative emotion or resistance you may be carrying, so that the energy that is within you can be in alignment with your desires.

When you align your energy and allow it to flow through you, with no resistance, you thrive in all ways. The results will absolutely amaze you.

March 13, 2004
ALLOWING

How much time do you spend talking about where you are…justifying why you are here and how you got here…looking and talking about what you don't want? Then you question why the things you do want don't come to you. The Law of Attraction states that whatever you give your attention to is what you constantly create in your life experience…and you keep creating more of what you focus upon.

As Abraham-Hicks says, "If you ask Magellan or any navigational system to plan a trip for you, you're given directions from where you are, directly to where you're going. They don't discuss where you've been in the past or where you might veer off into another direction…you aren't criticized for making a wrong turn. It just gives you directions to where you want to go, from where you are now."

Be your own navigational system with health issues, your body, relationships, careers, dollars…the way you feel, is an indication of what you're doing with your attention…your thoughts. To get the end result you would like to achieve, you have to be in alignment with what you want…to be a vibrational match with it. In other words, you have to feel as if you're already living it.

Get in alignment with your desires, look forward to where you want to go and don't keep looking back at where you've been and never justify where you are. Appreciate where you are as you become aware of how you feel, and be sensitive to that emotional guidance system within you, and look optimistically toward where you're going...putting your attention upon that which you are wanting, for as you choose the direction of your thought you are choosing the direction of your vibration. What you vibrate is ultimately what you create!

March 4, 2004
SELF-LOVE

We can only allow, into our lives, our personal opinion about "how I feel about me." It comes back to self-love and self-appreciation, which is our way of staying connected to that which we truly are...that wonderful, magnetic, spiritual being. We can only allow our good, to the amount that we love ourselves, and the vibration we're in.

There are times one has to listen to the statements that we make regarding ourselves. Listen to those negative ones in which we put ourselves down, i.e., "I'm not good enough...I'm too fat...I'm too thin...I'm not smart enough...I don't have enough money...I don't have the right education...I don't live in the right place...Why did I do that?...I don't get enough exercise."

It's not just one big situation that stops us from getting what we want. Think about some of the thoughts we think about and verbalize...it's a culmination of all those small negative thoughts and small negative things we say and do, all day long, everyday.

Whether it's about us or someone else or about some difficult situation…every time we have a thought that is negative in nature, in that one moment, those are the thoughts that are not allowing us to receive everything good. Those are the things we keep attracting.

Self-love is allowing love to flow through self. And love, flowing through self, feels like eagerness, passion, enthusiasm, glee and laughter. When you're feeling wonderful, you are allowing the purity of all that you consider to be good to flow through you. When you are suffering or feeling discomfort in any form, you are not allowing, for any reason.

Self-love has got to come from you…it's an inside job…it comes from the inside, out.

Within each of us is a loving, magical, powerful, true self!

February 19, 2004
HOW YOUR EMOTIONAL GUIDANCE SYSTEM WORKS

Many times, recently, when checking my e-mail, my virus protector has popped up telling me that it has deleted a negative, disabling virus before it can create a situation, which I would not want in my computer. As you may know, these viruses can destroy files or slow down the entire computer system. The virus protector can eliminate it or the virus can be quarantined so that it does no harm.

Doesn't this sound familiar? Every time we have a negative, disabling thought, which creates resistance we are, in fact, putting a virus in our system that does not serve us well, just like your computer.

Do you protect yourself from negative viruses as well as you protect your computer? Do you schedule regular "thought checkups"? Do you delete and repair, automatically, without interrupting your system with negative thought viruses? Do you provide yourself with a quick and easy system-recovery? Do you clean-sweep and use your wastebasket to clear out the internal emotional clutter?

When each negative thought virus appears, do you optimize your performance and solve your problems quickly with a click on the automatic delete icon, or do you allow those thought viruses to return over and over and over, until it gets so bad you have to quarantine them?

Do you feel, or are you sensitive to, your automatic emotional guidance system when it lets you know that you should be deleting a negatively infected thought, before it slows down your system, or creates something you don't want? Do you shift those negative infected thoughts, thus shifting them to thoughts that feel good?

Treat your emotional system as you would your computer...there are times when you just have to simply shut down your thoughts completely and re-boot to a new thought and a feeling that feels good to you, establishing a new vibration.

Your computer can only print out information you have entered into it, just as you can manifest only that which you think, feel and vibrate. The Universe serves only the vibration you have established.

Think and feel and look for the thoughts that feel good and, in this way, you automatically delete negative thoughts.

February 5, 2004
THOUGHTS AND FEELINGS

You are the allower of your experience. The way you feel is the indication of the degree of your point of focus or desire and your degree of allowing in the moment.

The way you feel and the thoughts you think are intricately combined, and it might be easier to feel your way to the success that you want, relative to whatever it is, rather than think your way there...just for a little while.

Life experience makes you think! People you talk with make you think! Things you think about make you think! Watching television makes you think! In other words, you're thinking all over the place...you are veritable thinkers...thinking, thinking, thinking. Now it's time to start, consciously, feeling in response to your thought. And if you find yourself feeling discord about a thought, change the thought. You have the power to do that.

Who you are is a free-feeling, empowering being. The way you feel lets you know what you are creating.

Remember...What you think, you feel–what you feel, you vibrate–what you vibrate, you create.   *94*

Let the way you feel be very important to you. The way you feel is the indicator of what you are doing with your thoughts and what you're ultimately creating. Go with the thoughts that feel best–that feel good–then you'll be the allower of your desires.

January 22, 2004
CREATING

You are a creator and contrast is the best stuff of the Universe because that's what helps creators know what it is they want.

Here is how it works: Here you are, examining the contrast, and out of it is born a new desire. Your work is to look at that new desire. Never mind what produced it, it is now a beginning place to create what you want.

With absolutely no resistance at all and no negative thought, think about what you want...imagine it...feel it like it's already here...feel joy and happiness...feel as if you are already living it and the Law of Attraction must bring you together, and manifestation then occurs.

Remember, what you think, what you remember, what you look at, what's in your imagination, what you're pondering or fantasizing about or thinking about...what you feel and what you create, are always a vibrational match.

Creating is about getting the feeling, and then you are allowing. Your contrast gives you the desire...your desire is what gives you the reason that you use to flow the energy. The flowing of the energy is the reason for the continuation of existence...the purpose is joy.

January 8, 2004
SHIFTING YOUR VIBRATION

New Year's Eve morning I was behind a car that had a bumper sticker which caught my attention. It read, "What if the 'Hokey-Pokey' IS what it's all about?" I chuckled, smiled and then thought, "That is, indeed, what it's all about." It's all about shifting and turning yourself about...from the negative thoughts to feelings that feel good to you, and just knowing that all is well.

The next time you find yourself caught up in that old habit of looking at and thinking about certain situations that do not please you, or if you're feeling fear, worry, doubt or frustration...any sort of negative emotion, feel the awareness to shift and turn yourself about with a new thought, a new feeling...reaching out for that which feels best, that which feels good...releasing resistance and allowing fully who you are. One who loves, who soars, who feels empowered, who enjoys living in the moment with all of life, be it work, play, relationships, travel, animals, children or nature...one who appreciates self as well as others, is feeling joy in every part of it.

What a wonderful way to begin a New Year...being aware of the signs all around that remind us of what it's all about...doing the "Hokey-Pokey," shifting and turning ourselves about, to allow all desires of well-being...feeling joy and having fun with it all.

December 23, 2003
FEELING JOY

It's the Season of Celebration with our loved ones...our loved ones in the physical world as well as those who have re-emerged back into the non-physical. So often, because we are feeling sadness about where we now stand in life, or, family situations which surround us, we don't allow ourselves to feel joy.

As we allow thoughts of appreciation, regarding where we are in the moment and see the beauty around us, as we celebrate the lives of our loved ones, both physical and non-physical, looking for joyful thoughts with love and laughter, they all join in and we feel the fullness of that...now that's a celebration!

Know that there is no separation. The Spirit of those you love, non-physically and physically, is always with you in the feeling of joy.

Feel the Spirit of the Holidays as a song in your heart, every day, allowing that feeling to touch everyone you come in contact with...taking you where your heart most wants to go...with all that brings you joy...that is the music to hear.

December 10, 2003
LAW OF ATTRACTION

All day long...every day, you are creating wanted desires or unwanted situations. You are launching, vibrationally, by how you are feeling, and the Universal forces are receiving these vibrations, and answering them. The Law of Attraction is managing all of it and your vibrations are always being answered. Only you know, by the way you feel, just what the Universe is answering.

There is magic in the Law of Attraction. It does not say that you are to ask...do all the right things, and then it will be given. Instead, it is telling you to ask and then don't offer contradictory thoughts to what you've asked for...just stop thinking negative thoughts.

Nothing is more exhilarating than to dance through life, recognizing that the Universe is there to yield to you whatever you want...whenever you want it. It's all about you! You get to choose it all, by the way you feel.

Everything you're experiencing is a mirror of the way you feel. So, how are you feeling? How do your thoughts feel??? Good or bad, only you can know.

Look around you at this time of year and enjoy this season, with its warmth, its merriment, its beautiful lights and music. Appreciate where you are in this moment and enjoy your NOW, as you pre-pave more of the "feel-good" thoughts and feelings, creating how you would like your life to be, day by day.

Everything you're living is a mirror of how you feel.

November 26, 2003
APPRECIATION

Appreciation is a powerful tool!

It is easy to see the negative side of almost anything. You have to choose just which side you want to deal with. If you are opting to see only those things you can appreciate (the allowing side), you are then using these moments to align yourself with Source. In doing so, you are allowing all things you consider to be good–not only those things you are actively appreciating, but all the things you desire.

What things are there for you to appreciate? A changing sky that never stops being more beautiful than the one before…nature in all its glory…the innocence of children…beloved pets…all creations and inventions, which do and will delight you…the eternal and never-ending supply of all things wanted.

There is no reason to ever feel anything other than love and appreciation and, if you should, for a brief moment, feel anything other than that…just step aside and look at that lovely sky or that child's smile and say, "How do I feel about what I am seeing?"…then, listen and feel for the unspeakable joy.

As we feel appreciation at this Thanksgiving season, know that appreciation is the feeling to feel, every day.

November 13, 2003
DOMINANT THOUGHTS AND FEELINGS

What negative thoughts and feelings do you continue to activate? If these thoughts and feelings become constant, or become habit, they will eventually become dominant, and whatever your dominant feeling is, will become your central point of attraction. In your humanness, you then feel that this is not something you would intentionally do to yourself…someone else must be responsible for the way you feel. Herein lies fact!!! You are doing every bit of it to yourself by continually practicing, over and over and over again, those same thoughts and feelings.

How do you change those "disallowing" thoughts and feelings? You have to practice different thoughts.

How do you let financial abundance become a more dominant feeling within you? You have to practice the thoughts and feelings that surround abundance. How do you let physical well-being become more dominant within you? You have to practice thoughts and feelings of well-being. You have to practice, practice, practice those good thoughts and feelings…you have to find thoughts that feel good to you, on subjects that are important to you, and try to stay tuned only to subjects that feel good.

If what you are thinking doesn't feel good, and you want to change…then change the subject.

You must stop thinking negative thoughts, about money, about relationships, about your physical condition, about your career, about anything you desire.

Simply activate another thought…one that feels good.

October 27, 2003
ART OF ALLOWING

The Art of Allowing means finding thoughts that feel good, about subjects that are important to you, in order to allow yourself to be a vibrational match to those things you're asking for. So, if there is anything you've been desiring that isn't showing up as quickly as you'd like it to…it is for one reason only, and that is that you're giving too much attention to how things are and not enough attention to how you would like things to be. Just make a decision that you're going to think only about thoughts that make you feel good.

Become an appreciator…for instance, try expressing a "Rampage of Appreciation," which only means that you intentionally look for things to appreciate whether they have anything to do with what you desire or not. Do it so deliberately that you actually take time to sit down with pen and paper and write it all down. Line after line, write down all the things you can think of to appreciate.

Instead of seeing things that are wrong to you or that you don't agree with, look for things which are very right to you and that you totally do agree with.

The best label you can put upon yourself is "I am an expert appreciator…I am an exaggerated appreciator…I always look for good things, wherever I am. It is my dominant intent to look for that which I can offer words of appreciation about," because in your attitude of appreciation, you align with who you are, and there can be no resistance to well-being and to your desires in that vibration.

October 16, 2003
BEING A VIBRATIONAL MATCH TO YOUR DESIRE

Usually, the reason you're not in a vibrational match with your own desire is because you've practiced thoughts that don't match it for so long that you can't seem to, easily, offer a thought that does match it.

You can't be thinking or worrying about not having enough dollars and then expect to be a vibrational match with attracting dollars.

You can't keep focusing on the negative, in a relationship or a past relationship, or what you don't want in a relationship, or the fact that the ideal relationship has not yet manifested for you, and expect to have what you desire, as that which you are focusing upon is not a vibrational match with your desire.

You can't keep thinking and worrying about illness or pain... about being fat or thin...short or tall...you can't keep giving your attention to that which you don't want, and yet be a vibrational match to that which you do want.

In other words, if you are not happy with a situation, you can't continue to give your attention to what is not wanted... be it dollars, your health, a satisfying career, wonderful relationships or whatever, and expect what you do want to manifest for you. They are just not a vibrational match with one another. You have to give your attention and feelings, (your focus), to what is desired in order to be a vibrational match with it...in order for you to attract it.

What is your dominant vibration (feeling) about life? Does it feel to you like freedom and excitement and anticipation toward that which is to come? Or does it feel like struggle and worry and uneasiness? You can tell by the way you feel if you are a vibrational match with your desires.

Only when you feel good do you have control of your vibrations, and then you are the deliberate creator of your own experience.

Let your criteria be: How does this thought feel?

October 2, 2003
EMOTIONS...VIBRATIONS

Optimism brings you so much, while pessimism keeps it from coming to you. Eagerness brings you so much, while disappointment keeps it from coming to you. Happy anticipation brings you so much, but disappointment keeps it from coming to you. Joy, love and appreciation all bring you so much, while anger, fear and depression keep it from coming to you.

The emotions you feel are indicators of whether you are a vibrational match with your desire or whether you aren't. Your emotions tell you what you are doing with your vibrational mix (your feelings). So, the happier you are, the more you are allowing what you really want to come to you. The unhappier you are, the more you are resisting the allowance of what you want to come to you. What you think and what you feel are what you vibrate and what you create, whether wanted or unwanted.

Look for thoughts that feel good!

September 18, 2003
PRE-PAVE YOUR DAY

When you waken from your sleep, your energy is always in a better, clearer place than it is in any point of your day, because while you slept, you reverted back into pure non-physical, and your energy has been sort of re-balanced.

With this new surge of energy, with your vibration at its very best, make a statement to yourself that you are going to look for more things that feel good to you. Begin to mentally pre-pave the day.

Throughout your day, if something happens that produces negative emotion, then process it to acknowledge the feeling and immediately pivot to something that you do want, and look for thoughts that feel good. Again, pre-pave how you want the rest of the day to be.

Be aware that the way you feel is the way you're vibrating and what you vibrate you create. Offer, many times a day, "I love feeling good...nothing is more important than that I feel good. Whatever I do, wherever I go, I'll look for reasons to feel good." Holding yourself in the vibration of feeling good enables you to allow all you've been asking for to flow to you.

You always have a choice in how you feel!

September 4, 2003
JOY

This is the recipe for eternal joy. It will, also, provide a format for a life of dramatic, magnificent creating:

> Seek reasons to offer words of praise, to yourself and to others!
> Seek beauty in nature, beasts and in humans!
> Seek reasons to love. In other words, in every segment of every day, look for something that brings forth, within you, a feeling of love!
> Seek only that which uplifts you!
> Seek the opportunity to offer, that which uplifts to another!
> Seek a feeling of well-being!

104

Know that your value can only be measured in terms of joy!!

Acknowledge your absolute freedom to do, or not to do, any of these things…for it is, without exception, your choice in every moment of every day.

When you keep your focus upon the joy, everything else will fall into place.

August 21, 2003
CONTRAST

Last Friday morning, I was shopping for some things at Office Max. As I was standing in quite a long line at the check-out, the woman in front of me was becoming very verbal and upset about the wait. She was loudly complaining about her discomfort and discontent, and the woman ahead of her joined the ruckus. As I noted all this uncomfortable confusion, I began to, mentally, shift my vibrations and appreciate the contrast they offered.

Every day we come across contrast and we always have a choice in how we handle it. We can join in, we can show either blame, or we can appreciate. My choice is to always appreciate, which then keeps me in a mode of feeling good.

The next time you come across a little contrast, remember that you have a choice in how you feel and what you want to give your attention to. Look for the positive aspects in all situations. Just appreciate and allow them. Take the path of least resistance, feeling your joy.

When you are in your joy, you are always on the right path.

August 7, 2003
FEELING GOOD

Everything that is happening to you is directly in response to what you think and feel. As you begin to let "feeling good" be your dominant quest, all things in your life will then begin to take shape according to those feelings.

Look at life this way: "What's out there–is there for whatever reason…it is what it is...but my life isn't at all about what's 'out there'…my life is about how I feel…so, right now, I am going to do my best to find a thought that feels good to me."

If you could "master" just one thing, let that single thing be how you feel–then all that you turn your attention to will become a satisfying experience.

JULY 10, 2003
WHAT ARE YOU GIVING YOUR ATTENTION TO?

A friend stopped by one day to drop something off and in the course of our conversation she said that the day was going to be an extremely busy one, and that her husband was not in the best of moods. I laughed and suggested that she keep her focus on feeling good, regardless, to look at her husband's positive aspects and begin to, mentally, pre-pave the day flowing with ease…to go on a rampage of appreciation with everything she could.

How often we get caught up in giving our attention to thoughts, conditions and situations of the moment that aren't necessarily what we would like them to be, instead of appreciating that moment and getting another thought that feels good…getting a new view, a new perception and looking for positive aspects.

If you let the condition or moods of OTHERS control the way you feel, you will always be trapped. But, when you're able to control the way you feel, because you control the thoughts you offer, then you ar truly liberated.

What are you giving your attention to??? What new thought do you need to offer???

June 26, 2003
YOU CREATE VIA YOUR THOUGHTS AND FEELINGS

Throughout your lifetime, anything that you experience has, and will have, only the meaning you give it...you give your permission for what you experience...so, look for the positive aspects.

What you are living today is a direct result of the thoughts and feelings that you have felt before this time. Your future is created from where your viewpoint is in this moment.

Your power is in your now and you are only a thought away from feeling good!

June 12, 2003
FEELING GOOD IS NATURAL TO YOU

It is natural for you to feel good!
It is natural for you to have life treat you right!
It is natural for you to live life with abundance!
It is natural for you to live well-being!
It is natural for you to love and be loved!

Go about your day and practice that which is natural for you. When you find yourself remembering and rehashing any thoughts that you feel resistance to (which is evidenced by negative emotion), just laugh about it. Make fun of yourself and tell yourself that you are now going to relax a little and allow the energy to flow.

Begin to ask yourself, "What am I giving my attention to?" or, "What thought am I thinking, that is keeping me from living what is so natural to me?" Then, get a new thought…a new view…a new perception to live what is natural to you.

There is no way it will not get better and better and better.

May 29, 2003
HOW YOU FEEL IS HOW YOUR LIFE IS

The Universe says, "If that's the way you feel…then that's the way it is." So, if you feel abundance and prosperity, that's the way you feel, and that's the way it is. If you feel healthy, that's the way you feel and that's the way it is. If you feel happy, that's the way you feel and that's the way it is.

Think thoughts that make you feel good…Speak words that make you feel good…Get the feeling of how you would like your life to be…Get the feeling as if you're already living that life.

Feel it–feel it–feel it. Feel the way you want to feel, ON PURPOSE…this **is** what the Universe responds to.

May 15, 2003
LAUGHTER IS PURE, POSITIVE ENERGY

Laughing is the physical embodiment of pure, positive energy. It is the sound of your Inner Being, (your spirit), coming forth into the physical. It is the way you felt when you first came forth. When one becomes almost out of control with joyous laughter, one is translating the energy of his/her Inner Being into the perfect human physical words of outrageous and uncontrollable joy.

In all areas of your life, it is through your joy that success comes to you...NOT through your struggle.

Laugh your way to success...thought by thought by thought!!!

May 1, 2003
POSITIVE FEELINGS-VIBRATIONS-AND ALLOWING

If you're feeling unworthy, you can work day and night, night and day, every day, and not allow the very things that you want to flow to you, because your vibration is not allowing it, and the Universe can't buck your current.

You can feel good about the flower you're looking at...the ocean you're looking across...the smile on a happy child's face, or enjoy the good feeling you achieve just by petting your pet. If you can be focused upon something like that, and feel utter well-being, then, in that moment of basking, you are attracting the dollars you want, the abundance of all things that you want...you are attracting the mate that you want and the good health that you want. You are attracting whatever it is that you truly desire. You see, it's about vibrating and allowing.

You don't have to work at your high vibration. Your higher, purer vibration is natural to you. But, you do have to let go of the thoughts and feelings that are holding your vibration down.

The better you feel–the more you are allowing!

April 17, 2003
INFLUENCE

Our most common weakness is our habit of leaving our minds open to the negative influence of others. Most are affected by the words of others, rather than by our own experiences.

Others may believe differently, may choose differently, may want differently, and may act differently. When we realize and recognize that the only thing that affects us is what we are doing with our own feelings...our own vibrations...that no one else can vibrate for us...that we are the only one to have any power in our experience, allowing all others their differences and yet choosing to feel good anyway, then we can move forward freely and joyously.

When you are looking, be it in the past, the present or the future...always look for that which feels good to you.

April 3, 2003
LIVING IN THE MOMENT

As you presently view events which you deem unwanted, be they personal or worldwide, there is a tendency to let whatever you are viewing become more important than is really necessary, because everything is constantly changing in response to whatever vibration you are emitting.

Can you feel the advantage you have in knowing that you are the creator of your own experience? And, can you feel the advantage you have in the knowledge of what your emotions mean?

Can you feel how good it is that you know what the path of least resistance feels like and that you can discover more in every day how easy it is to take that path?

Why would anyone want to choose the path of least resistance??? Because when you're not resisting good...Good Is!

Make no mistake that the path of least resistance and the path of most allowance are identical paths. Allowance of what? Allowance of Source, clarity, wellness, abundance, good feeling, love, appreciation, lovers, friends, compliments, well-being of all manner...that's what you are allowing when you are reaching for thoughts that feel good.

Use your time wisely, spending more of it creating, speculating, dreaming, imagining and envisioning, and let your observation be about looking for things that feel good, rather than weighing the pros and cons. Let the guidance that comes forth from within be so important that if anything doesn't feel good to you, try your best to distract yourself as quickly as possible.

The basis for your life is freedom...in fact, you're so free you can choose to direct your thoughts anywhere you choose...so let feeling good be what matters the most, let joy be your quest...then expansion or growth will be the natural result of your being focused.

Realize the power of now.

March 20, 2003
CREATIVE VISUALIZATION

You can't keep giving your attention to what you do not want and expect life to change!

You can't keep talking about how things are and create change. Appreciate where you are for showing you what you do or do not want. If you were going to do some re-decorating around the house or the office, would you keep mentally seeing it as it is or would you begin to see it differently, as you would like it to be?

If your vision of it is only as it presently is, you do not change it. When you envision it differently, you then attract that change to you. It is the same with all things in your life experience...you have to see things as you would like them to be, for any change to be made...not how they presently are...see it differently...in a different light, be it personal or world events.

Look for the positive aspects in all situations...Appreciate you and all of life...meditate and focus on more Harmony–Happiness–Success and Abundance in all areas of life, be it physical, career or relationships. Do this for yourself as well as the entire world and experience life with joy and freedom, connecting with Source as the Universe responds purely to your expectation.

March 8, 2003
YOUR POINT OF ATTRACTION

What you feel, you vibrate and spread to the Universe, and that attracts back to you. When you feel joy, you spread joy, and attract more joy…when you feel love, you spread love, and that attracts more love…when you feel appreciation, you spread appreciation, and attract to you more appreciation…when you feel happy, you spread happiness, and you attract more happiness…when you spread abundance, you attract more abundance. How you feel about any subject is what you will attract back into your experience.

It's not about what others do or don't do…it's about how you feel about what they do or don't do. It's all about how you are feeling. If you want something…how do you feel about your choice??? Be it bad or good, beautiful or ugly, happy or sad, how you feel is what you spread and which ultimately you will attract. How you feel is your point of attraction!!!

How are you feeling now? What are you feeling…spreading…attracting?

February 20, 2003
HABITS…OF THOUGHTS, FEELINGS AND VIBRATIONS

If there's something you want that's not coming to you, it's only for one reason: you are vibrationally different from it. If you have something you don't want, it's because you are vibrationally the same as it is. Why you vibrate differently from your desire is because of your habits of observations, your habits of thoughts and your habits of feelings.

What you are experiencing is a reflection of what you are observing, thinking and feeling. What you are thinking, feeling and observing is reflected in your vibration, and those vibrations are what the Universe is accepting as your point of attraction. What the Universe is accepting as your point of attraction becomes your future manifestation.

If your one goal in life was to have only thoughts that feel good...you could live life successfully and happily on the way to fulfilling your heart's desires.

February 6, 2003
VIBRATIONAL HARMONY

This Universe is energy-based and it is all about vibration. Law of Attraction is managing it and if you want something, you must be in a vibrational match to it. It is as simple as that.

Simply stated: when you desire something, and you're feeling eagerness, joy appreciation or passion...in those feelings of positive emotion, you're in a receiving mode. And as you maintain that reception, you'll be the full receiver of that which you are asking for.

But, if you're feeling fear or vulnerability, anger, revenge, blame, guilt or any of what can be described as negative emotions, simply put...you are not in a receiving mode of good things, and you can't let them into your experience as long as you feel that way.

The secret of creating anything that you want is to get happy and stay there...because in your joy, you are always in the place of allowing that which is in vibrational harmony with who you are and what you are wanting.

January 23, 2003
SETTING YOUR VIBRATIONAL TONE

The most important choice you have is how you feel. How you feel is your vibration, and that vibration is what you radiate and emit to the Universe. Through the Law of Attraction that then is attracted back to you and becomes your life experience.

Your vibration is your power of influence…and as you deliberately and consciously focus only on thoughts that make you feel good, each day you will have established your "vibrational tone" to your pure, positive Source energy. And, after a few short weeks of this concentrated effort you will find yourself becoming a living, eating, breathing light being.

You are always only one thought away from feeling good!

January 9, 2003
SHIFT YOUR VIBRATION…NOW

Every time you're tempted to react, think or feel in the same old way, ask yourself if you want to be a prisoner of your past or the pioneer of your future.

Where you now stand is a direct result of the thoughts and feelings that you've offered before, but, where you're going is a direct result of the perspective you hold now.

Life is a series of now, now, now moments. Shift your thoughts and feelings and create your now and your future…to be, to do and to have all that you desire.

December 19, 2002
SETTING YOUR INTENTIONS

Excerpts from "Sara 3," by Esther and Jerry Hicks (Abraham-Hicks Publications)

The way life is supposed to feel, in every moment, is perfect and expanding. Enough–but becoming more...Satisfied–but eager for something else...Complete–but never finished.

You live in a big world with many other people, who may want things to be different than you want them to be. You cannot convince them all to agree with you and you cannot coerce them into agreeing with you. Your only path to a joyous, powerful experience is to decide, once and for all, that you intend to feel good, no matter what. And, as you practice turning your thoughts to things that do feel good...now you have discovered the secret to life.

Wishing you a happy and joyous Holiday Season...

December 5, 2002
POINT OF ATTRACTION

You are not affected by what other people do. What you think about what other people do is what affects you.

No matter how justified you may be in your negative emotions, anytime you're feeling ANY negativity, your point-of-attraction is attracting all kinds of things you don't want in your now and/or in your future.

So...wherever you are looking...be it past, present or future, look for that which feels good!

November 21, 2002
APPRECIATION

Rampage of Appreciation: Appreciation is a pure positive energy vibration that matches that thing which you want in your experience. It feels good in your powerful and important now, it guarantees wonderful future experiences, and the Universe responds to it over and over and over again.

It is most important to appreciate yourself, because the way you feel about you is your very basis of attraction. Take a moment and go on a real Rampage of Appreciation, appreciating everyone and everything in your life. Do it because of who you are…because you are an appreciator.

As your appreciation grows, so will its rewards. As you connect to your natural state of appreciation, you will experience Thanksgiving every day of your life.

November 7, 2002
FEELING JOY

What you do every day…what you say, how you think and how you feel will do more to shape the future of your life and your country than any other single factor.

The important thing is to feel joy and just spread it everywhere you can…as often as you can…as loudly as you can…as much as you can and as far as you can.

October 22, 2002
APPRECIATION

When you are not loving and appreciating, you are less than who you really are. The natural state of well-being is that of feeling joy and feeling good. Anything other than that is not natural.

Appreciate everything in your life. Don't appreciate because of any one or any thing, appreciate because of who you are, because you are an appreciator, you are a lover. Don't let anyone or anything take you from who you are, or from your grace. Don't play at loving and appreciating, really do it and get the feeling of it.

Where does it begin? Where does it originate? From you!

Remember...The Universe isn't playing Halloween tricks on you–How you think and how you feel are what you vibrate to the Universe and that is what the Universe returns...that is your creation!

October 8, 2002
THOUGHTS THAT FEEL GOOD

Speak from your perspective, "I'm a really good person. I've made a wonderful choice in coming into this physical experience at this time. Everyone else around me is also really good. We have all come forth with powerful, clear and loving intentions, and well-being is the order of our day...whether we are recognizing that it's where we are standing or not."

"Today, no matter where I'm going...no matter what I'm doing...no matter who I'm with, it is my dominant intent to look for the thought that feels best, within the range of my vision...because nothing is more important than that I feel good; when I'm feeling good, I'm in the state of allowing all of this wonderful stuff that I so much want and deserve."

August 27, 2002
SCRIPTING

You are the director of your own movie. You get to write all of the parts…you get to write the parts of everyone who plays with you…how they respond to you…how you feel about them and how they feel about you. But, you do it with your vibrational language, not your language of words or actions.

Your now is powerful. The only thing that affects your experience is your vibration, and your vibration reaches to the boundaries of the Universe. Where you are is the result of thoughts that you have thought up to this point.

The thoughts and feelings you have in your now are very powerful and no matter where you may be in your frustrated state, if you alter your vibration, the Universe will respond and your new movie will be created.

Create a joyous day!

Love and appreciation,

Linda

The "Thoughts from Linda" are inspired by Abraham-Hicks

Glossary of terms

A

Abraham – Abraham is a group of non-physical teachers who have brought their message to us via Esther and Jerry Hicks of San Antonio, Texas.

Abundance – Abundance is your natural state of well-being, when you are positively connected to your Source. Prosperity (money, success, fame, possessions) is a creative by-product of this well-being and frequently is evidence of how you flow your energy toward what you desire.

Appreciation – Appreciation means looking for the positive in something without resistance. It is the purest and strongest form of unconditional love.

C

Contrast – Contrast is an important step in the creation process. Contrast is looking at what you don't want. It assists you in identifying what you do want. Contrast fine tunes your conclusions about what you really want and causes the passion that you need to move your thoughts and feelings to the vibrational place you need to be in, to create.

Creative Process – You create by how you think and feel.

Creative Visualization – Creative visualization is a tool or process to assist you to flow your energy by imaging or imagining what you want to create.

120

D

Default –In default, you are creating without realizing what your role is in the process. Default is also what occurs when negative emotions have been with you for so long that you accept them as normal and create from a negative place.

Dominant Thoughts and Beliefs – A dominant thought or belief is just a well-practiced thought. It is a thought that you keep thinking. It is a habit.

Disallowing Energy – Disallowing energy is the "pinching off" or "crimping" of the energy stream.

E

Emotions – Emotions are pure non-physical energy, guiding you via your Inner Being or inner guidance. Positive emotion is evoked when you are feeling good, and negative emotion occurs when you are feeling bad. Emotions are your guideposts for making adjustments.

Energy – Energy is vibration. Everything is energy, and life is about the flow of that energy.

F

Fear – Fear is an emotion and dominant belief that something negative will happen, or that something will not happen.

Feelings – Feelings are the vibrational reading of, or the response to, your thoughts.

Flowing Energy – Flowing energy is how you use energy to create. You are an electronic transmitter and receiver of Source energy and what flows from you is what you receive in return, thus creating your experience.

Focusing – Focusing is giving your attention to any subject or event with intensity and limited distraction.

I

Inner Guidance – Your inner guidance is your Inner Being (your guidance system) or your "soul." It is pure, positive, non-physical Source energy, and you are an extension of that.

J

Journaling – Journaling is the act of writing down your thoughts and feelings.

Joy – Joy is your life's quest. It is bringing forth from within you a feeling of well-being.

K

Knowing – You are born with a "knowing." It is the understanding, or your vibrational harmony with, non-physical energy.

L

Lack – Lack is your denial of an abundant Universe and the non-allowing of non-physical energy. Lack is the erroneous thinking that there is never enough, and that if someone else has it, you can't have it, too.

M

Meditation – Meditation is a tool or process that is used to clear your mind of vibrational resistance. Various processes can be utilized to achieve a meditative state.

Missing Link – The "missing link," spiritually speaking, is not connecting fully with the energy of your Inner Being or your inner guidance (your soul–the non-physical, spiritual you), and allowing the Universal Energy to flow through you.

122

N

Non-Physical – Non-physical energy is the Universal stream of vibrations or consciousness, the creative life-force, the God-force, All That Is, or whatever name you want to call it. We are all an extension of this non-physical energy; it flows through you as your life force, and connects you to All That Is.

P

Positive Aspect Book – A positive aspect book is a book in which you record the things you are looking at in a positive way. It is a tool to help maintain positive energy.

Pre-Paving – Pre-paving is a tool or process that assists you to pre-plan how you want something to be. It is a way that you set the tone, in advance, to use your energy more deliberately.

Prosperity – Prosperity is a creative by-product of joy. (See "Abundance")

R

Resistance – Resistance is basically "negative emotion." Or more clearly, resistance is a "stubborn negative emotion." It is pushing against. Resistance is a disconnection to the Source of your creative energy.

S

Scripting – Scripting is a process of writing something on paper, which allows you to tell the Universe the way you want something to be, as if it is already happening. It gets you into the feeling place of your desires by way of a "story."

Shifting Your Energy – Shifting your energy is seeing a situation in a different way, in order to remove resistance.

Source Energy – The Source of the energy that comes into the Universe, which is All That Is, or the God-force, or whatever name you want to give to it. It is the same energy that created the earth, and it flows forth constantly.

T

Thoughts – A thought is focused consciousness. It is a vibrational signal that is used to request a creative response from Source energy.

U

Unconditional Love – Unconditional love is allowing love to flow through you without reservation.

Universal Energy – There is one stream of pure, positive energy, defined as non-physical, Universal, the God-force, All That Is, or whatever name you want to give it. You are connected to this Universal stream of non-physical energy since it flows through you. It is your life force.

Universal Laws – There are three Universal creational laws that cannot be changed or rewritten and which encompass the beginning and the end of the creative process. They are: The Law of Attraction, The Law of Deliberate Creation and The Law of Allowing.

V

Vibration – Vibrations are pulsations or reverberations that manifest chemically as energy. Vibrations are how you feel, and how you feel is what directs your creative process.

W

Well-Being – The feeling of well-being comes from being in vibrational harmony with your Source. It is a by-product of feeling joy. It is your natural state of being.

Resource guide

Linda Fallucca: www.lindafallucca.com for upcoming events and archived "Thoughts from Linda;" or, contact lindafallucca@ameritech.net to be added to future bi-weekly "Thoughts from Linda" e-mail messages. You may write to Linda at: P.O. Box 1083, Northbrook, IL 60065-1083; Phone: 847-272-9465.

Abraham-Hicks: www.abraham-hicks.com Write for information about the Abraham-Hicks "Science of Deliberate Creating/Art of Allowing" workshops, and to receive a brochure of available tapes, CDs, and books: Esther and Jerry Hicks, P.O. Box 690070, San Antonio, TX 78269; Phone: (830) 755-2299; FAX: (830) 755-4179.